Haiti Beyond Belief

Frank J. Nice, RPh, DPA, CPHP

© Copyright 2017

Nice Breastfeeding, LLC

7409 Algona Court

Derwood, MD 20855

301-840-0270 phone

301-840-0270 fax

www.NiceBreastfeeding.com

Library of Congress Control Number:

ISBN-13:9780998502410

Table of Contents

Haiti Beyond Belief

Frank J. Nice

Forward

On October 4, 2016, the eye of Hurricane Matthew (Mathieu in Haiti) passed almost directly over the towns of Leon and Carcasse in Haiti with winds of over 140 miles per hour and heavy downpours. The school/orphanage, the children's health clinic, the second school, the church, and the clinic we service are in Leon. In addition, the school, the church, and the clinic we service are in Carcasse.

In Leon, the church was heavily damaged completely, losing its roof, and the school/orphanage also was heavily damaged by wind and water, with the school/orphanage losing its roof. The children's health clinic, with having just spent $25,000 to build it, was heavily damaged. The children and orphans were left without shelter, clothing, food, and water. In Carcasse, the church was completely destroyed and the school lost its top floor, with reported deaths. Both towns saw over 80% destruction of homes, complete devastation of trees and foliage, including the coffee industry, and catastrophic destruction of the animal population. Cholera has now viciously resurfaced.

We have received constant, impassioned pleas from Brother Fosy, Pere Jeanot, and Pere Verdieu for food and aid and assistance, both monetary and non-monetary. The situation has become overwhelming for both our Haitian brothers and sisters and for those of us trying to come up with assistance.

Even weeks after the hurricane, the US Government, the Red Cross, Catholic Relief Services, nor anyone of their ilk has set foot in Leon or Carcasse. Nothing has changed since the hurricane for the Haitian people despite being hammered disaster after disaster. The United

Nations despite finally admitting bringing cholera to Haiti after being exposed, now claims immunity from any Haitian claims for indemnity. Except for what we are trying to do personally to help the Haitian people, they are basically on their own as always. Everything in Haiti still remains beyond belief.

Introduction

It has been almost 20 years since my first trip to Haiti. I had just presented at a conference on the use of medication during breastfeeding and was attending a dinner that the conference sponsors were hosting for the speakers. Approximately eight of us were enjoying our food when one of the attendees brought up the topic of "White privilege." She is a Black woman who had spoken at the conference on breastfeeding in the Black population in the United States. My ears perked up, and I thought immediately about growing up in a poor coal mining town in Pennsylvania where my two Polish-born grandfathers had worked the coal mines and ended up dying from the effects of Black (ironic terminology) Lung Disease. My father was fortunate enough to drive a coal truck with his sixth-grade education and only had lingering effects of Black Lung Disease. He would later die from Parkinson's disease instead. Because of the work ethic shown by my grandparents and my parents, I was the first in my extended family to go to college to get a degree. I earned a BS in Pharmacy. My thoughts were, "What 'White privilege' did my family and I 'inherit?'"

Those thoughts ground to a halt when the woman then stated: "If you say you are *not* a racist, you are a racist." Therefore, I had two obvious responses to this declaration:

1. I am a racist (affirmed by statement of fact).
2. I am *not* a racist (affirmed by inference).

Of course, no matter what response I gave, I would condemn myself to being a racist.

I then pondered that there had to be another response, thinking what it would be.

1. I have a lot of Black friends. Then, I thought that whenever someone is accused of being a racist, this is the first

statement one makes in defense. It is usually dismissed because it is possible to have many Black friends and still be racist. Not adequate "proof."

2. I am married to a Korean woman. This was better, but still not enough "proof." Even though my wife is a "woman of color" and a "minority," she is not a Black woman. I could still be racist when it comes to Blacks.

3. One of my daughters is married to a Black man, and I have three Black grandchildren.
Once again, this is probably not sufficient "proof." My daughter made the choice to marry a Black man; it was not my choice. It had to be my choice.

4. It was then that I thought about my medical missions to Haiti over the past 20 years. I did not have to "say" that I was *not* a racist to affirm that I was, in fact, a racist, by the Black woman speaker's inference. It would be my body, mind, and soul actions that would affirm that I was not, in fact, a racist. In addition, if that were possible for one person, it was then possible for others.

Growing up in a typical middle-class family in the small coal-mining town of Plymouth, Pennsylvania, I only knew of one Black family that had ever lived in my town. All I can remember is that the man had been some kind of famous athlete. I did not meet another Black individual until I went to a special summer course at Bucknell University in Lewisburg, Pennsylvania for students who had excelled in high school. It was not until one year later when I attended Temple University in Philadelphia that I became immersed in the Black community. Never in my whole life, basically spent in that small coal-mining town, did I ever think I would end up ever going to a country such as Haiti.
I had been out of Pennsylvania only once in my life.

As a public health pharmacist, I have written four other books in my lifetime on breastfeeding, pregnancy, and medications. Over that time, I have been encouraged by friends to write about my experiences in Haiti. As close in miles and air time as is the poorest country in the world to the richest country in the world, so little is known about what it is like to live in Haiti.

It is because of the challenge of the Black speaker at the breastfeeding conference and because of the encouragement of my friends that I write this book. Haiti, indeed, is a country beyond belief, but it is also a country that is not beyond faith in God and beyond hope in their fellow human beings, whatever their race or color.

Chapter 1

Haiti

Haiti at a Glance

It is impossible to visualize the poverty and desolation prevalent throughout Haiti unless you are able to personally witness these images. In the literature, we read that Haiti is among the poorest and least developed countries in the world. Its poor infrastructure, lack of healthcare, and political turmoil perpetuate an environment that is defined by social instability and the uncertainty of whether improvements in medical care and social structure will ever occur. The suffering and long-term consequences in this community resulting from environmental disasters and a long history of government instability have not offered an easy solution to uplift this island from poverty and despair.

Subsequent to the earthquake that struck Haiti on January 12, 2010, Haiti was left with widespread destruction and a death toll of more than 200,000 people. Additionally, the earthquake forced over two million individuals to become homeless, with as many as 500,000 still without homes. Six years later, the aftermath continues to plague the island, especially in the many tent cities that emerged in response to the need for shelter for those who had lost their homes in the earthquake. The blue tarp tents are now gone, but I am not sure where their inhabitants went. The earthquake homes still exist in their original state and are too dangerous to inhabit. These communities provide testimony of the extreme poverty and serve as the epitome of the struggles that Haiti is continuing to endure. For those who have never travelled to Haiti, no photograph will be able to truly capture the pain, violence, and death that define the country.

An element of heightened concern that clouds the minds of those worldwide is the devastating state of the existing healthcare system.

The longstanding inadequacies in healthcare, education, and social stability have resulted in high illiteracy and unemployment rates, scarcity of clean water and electricity, malnutrition, and unsanitary conditions. These conditions fail to promote and ensure good health and exacerbate the stresses that illness and death have continued to impose on the country. To further illustrate the effects of a failed system, according to the World Health Organization, the average life expectancy in Haiti is 61 years old for men and 63 years old for women as compared to 76 years old for men and 81 years old for women in the United States. Furthermore, Haiti has the highest rates of infant and maternal mortality in the Western hemisphere with diarrhea, respiratory infections, malaria, tuberculosis, and HIV/AIDS being the leading causes of death.

My Personal History of Haiti

Almost every time I return home from Haiti and describe the conditions there, I am asked how Haiti can be so bad. Why do the Haitians not do anything to help themselves? Why do the Haitians allow these conditions to exist? It is not the purpose of my reflections to deal with these questions and issues. One can read many textbooks and novels that explain and confront these issues, especially the role of the United States and other countries, such as France and the Dominican Republic, in Haiti's history and condition.

The Defeat of Victory

There is another part of Haiti's history that I have a personal and cultural interest. As I stated, my grandparents came from Poland to work the coal mines of Pennsylvania. My Polish forefathers also came to Haiti, and their descendants still live there. This is the brief story of Haiti and the Polish Legionnaires:

In the many years that I have been to Haiti, what is extraordinary has been the handful of times I have come face to face with blue-eyed (oh, how those blue eyes shine and reflect back into your heart and soul) Haitian or a Haitian with a Polish-sounding name. There is even a village in Haiti called Kasel (Cazale). How did that ever happen?

Haiti was the third country in the world in 1804 to establish a democratic form of government after the world's only successful slave revolution (except for the Jews under Moses). The first democratic government was the United States in 1776, followed by Poland in 1779. How is that for a democratic triumvirate: United States, Poland, and Haiti? During the years to follow, all three nations became intertwined in political intrigue—good and bad.

In 1804, the black slaves of Haiti rose up and went to war against Napoleon and his French army. When the French forces came to Haiti to suppress the revolution and to fight against the slaves, there were 5,200 Polish officers and Legionnaires aligned with the French army.

The Poles were astonished and horrified by the way the Blacks were oppressed, brutalized, ill-equipped, and out-numbered by the French troops. Most of the Polish Legionnaires defected and decided to fight with the Haitian slaves against the Napoleonic forces. Eventually, the Haitian slaves and Polish Legionnaires defeated Napoleon's soldiers, and Haiti became a free and independent democratic nation.

The conflict cost over 4,000 of the Polish Legionnaires their lives. To make matters worse for the Polish Legionnaires, once the French army lost the war, it returned to France. Many of the surviving Polish Legionnaires were abandoned to stay in Haiti with no way out. They settled in Kasel (Cazale), Jacmel, and Fond des Blancs. They intermarried with Haitian women, and Polish descendants are still there 210 years later. Even though Polish is no longer spoken, there are still those who have Polish names. Maybe, if you are Polish, just maybe, you will travel to Haiti and meet a fellow Pole.

Chapter 2

My Haitian Friends (Zanmi Mwen)

I could flat out say that all Haitians are my friends, and in a way, that would be true, but of course, I cannot meet every Haitian, and even if I could, not everyone would be my friend. I do have some very special and dear friends in Haiti that I want to profile to show what down to earth (as I like to call my Pennsylvania friends) people they are.

The Three Peres (Fathers/Priests/Pastors)

Pere Jean Antoine

When I arrived in Haiti for my first mission trip to Leon, Haiti, Pere Jean Antoine was the new pastor of St. Paul's Church. He spoke broken English, and I spoke broken-down Creole. Despite this, we seemed to understand just about everything we said to each other. Pere Jean Antoine appeared to be a big man to me compared to other Haitian men that I had already met. Now when I see him, he does not look so big in stature, although he has not changed his body shape. Another thing that I noticed was that when I shook his hand for the first time, his hand was rough and calloused. I had shaken the hands of other priests, and their hands were soft and smooth. I was later told by a friend that if the pastor's hands were rough, they were truly pastors of the people. These were the pastors who drove motorbikes or road donkeys to travel far distances; these were the pastors that were your chauffeurs at your calling; these were the pastors that were carpenters, electricians, plumbers, laborers, and gardeners on the side; these were the pastors who saw themselves no better than their fellow man. Pere Jean Antoine proved to be just that kind of pastor, priest, and man. We have become lifelong friends.

When I arrived at St. Paul's Church on this first trip to Haiti, I readily noticed that Pere Jean Antoine did not have a whole lot to work with materially. He gave up his room so we could sleep more comfortably; he gave up his place and food at the table so we could eat more suitably; and he gave up his toilet and shower so that we could feel more at home. He was basically isolated from the outside world at most times as his shortwave radio only functioned sporadically. He was in possession of a rundown clinic building with a pharmacy that looked like Old Mother Hubbard's cupboard. There was no running water or functioning toilet, very little light was able to enter the dark and dank interior of the building, the roof leaked, and it was cold and damp inside despite the fact that it was in Haiti! I had never seen a "clinic" and "pharmacy" like this in my life. Not knowing what to expect on my first trip to Haiti, being a pharmacist, I had collected several duffel bags of drug samples (yes; there was a time when samples were readily available to pharmacists in the United States). From what I recall, some were even out of date (not much of an issue back then as something was better than nothing, the drugs were not that much out of date, and I knew their quality was still good). I met the resident nurse at the pharmacy, and we "stocked" the shelves with the contents of the duffel bags. Once on the shelves, the shelves looked pretty much empty as before we "filled" them. I looked at the nurse and asked her how long the supply would last. She responded, "One week."

When I was done, I went back to Pere Jean Antoine and said that this cannot be. I would be back again next year, and I would come back for a whole week with a medical team and drugs. This had never happened before in Leon. There had never been a medical team in Leon. The vast majority of people in Leon and its vast mountain, jungle area had never seen a doctor or pharmacist. Pere Jean Antoine made it his commitment on the spot to do whatever it took to make the medical mission a reality despite the realities of life outside of the clinic. Over the succeeding years, he lived up to this commitment and many others. He vowed that he would learn to speak English fluently so that he could work and communicate more easily with us in the future. That he did, and the next time we visited, he was able to communicate with us with adequate, sound English.

The next year that we came back with our medical team, the clinic looked very different. It was not a state-of-the-art clinic like what is seen in the United States, but it was vastly improved. The toilet was functioning and the water was running. It was not exactly clean and potable water, but it was running. We were provided potable boiled water for ourselves and for mixing our patients' medications. The leaks in the roof in some of the rooms were repaired so that we now had some usable rooms to see patients. The veranda was restored to provide an area out of the rain for triaging patients. The windows were now able to admit enough light during the day to see what we were doing, even if it did not allow air in. Benches were provided for patients to sit on. One room was restored to make it the living quarters for a Haitian missionary brother, Fosy Josil, who had befriended Pere Jean Antoine. There will be more on this man, who at that time was a mysterious stranger.

Pere Jean remains my dear friend 21 years since the day we first met. He has visited the United States to have dinner with my wife, Myung, and me. He has moved on from Leon and has been pastor at several churches. He is now pastor of Dame Marie's Catholic Church in the Grand Anse. On every trip to or from Port-au-Prince to our Carcasse mission, I always stop to visit with Pere Jean Antoine. He always asks how Myung is and remembers the great Korean meal that she prepared for him. He remains the hard-working, humble, compassionate, down-to-earth man and pastor that I met many years ago and has aged like fine wine.

Pere Verdieu

After building up and maintaining the Leon medical mission and clinic for 15 years, I felt an urge to move on to new grounds and to see where else in Haiti medical help was drastically needed. The mission in Leon to me was now on "automatic." Medical teams were now showing up on schedule three times a year. The opportunity to start a new medical mission in Carcasse, Haiti opened up. Leon was approximately a one- hour vehicle trip to Jeremie, the closest city, over not so great roads (the term is used loosely). Carcasse was four hours away on the far seacoast of northwest Haiti on roads that literally disappeared at times. The people of Carcasse were even poorer than those of Leon. The pastor of St. Joseph's Church in Carcasse was and still is Pere Verdieu. I met Pere Verdieu the first time when we arrived in Carcasse very late at night for our very first medical mission there in 2010.

Pere Verdieu was of a slighter build than Pere Jean Antoine, but he was very strong in appearance. When I shook his hand, it was the same rough hand that Pere Jean Antoine presented to me. I knew I had met a similar man in work ethic, and it proved true. Pere Verdieu was also an on-call chauffeur, but with different driving talents than Pere Jean Antoine. He could get a vehicle through any situation other than a definitive life-threatening one. At one time, we approached a nearly impassable, partially flooded-out, very muddy cow pasture-like road. None of the professional drivers could get their vehicles through. We were so close to our destination and yet so far. Pere Verdieu finally got out of the vehicle he was driving in his priestly clothes and nicely shined shoes and walked in ankle deep mud to the first vehicle. He got in and drove it out and at times above the mud to the other side of the stream. He then walked back two more times to drive the other two vehicles across. Pere Verdieu was also an all-around handyman, carpenter, plumber, electrician, and laborer. One morning, one of the women on the medical mission team clogged up the only available toilet. Pere Verdieu stuck his hand down the toilet drain hole but could not unclog the toilet. He then removed the whole toilet to expose the drain hole, cleared out the clog, reset the toilet, and then cemented it back to the floor. It took Pere Verdieu all of one hour to accomplish this feat.

Yet, for all their similarities, Pere Verdieu was unlike Pere Jean Antoine in many ways. Pere Verdieu is a pure businessman, as well as a pastor, and knows a good deal when he can get it. He does this to get the best he can for the members of his church as well as for the whole town of Carcasse. He will get every cent he can out of the medical team with his fees for this and for that service, but it's not for his own selfish gain. It is always for his people. His honesty is what you would expect of a pastor with rough, hard hands. Because of this approach to his work and dealings with people, Pere Verdieu was and is a tough partner to work with in Haiti. The best way is to get everything in writing and signed off so each party knows exactly where it stands and exactly what the terms of the contract are. Pere Verdieu is more like the modern businessman whereas Pere Jean Antoine is more like the businessman of my father's day, where a verbal agreement and a handshake were all that was needed to seal a deal and honor a commitment. No doubt about it though, both Pere Verdieu and Pere Jean Antoine know the obstacles and barriers and harsh realities of getting something done in Haiti and use their best God-given talents to make it happen.

Pere Pierre Jeanot

I have known Pere Pierre Jeanot for only a few years. He is the current pastor in Leon. Several pastors with fairly short stays in Leon followed Pere Jean Antoine. Since I have spent much of my time and effort in Carcasse during those years, I never developed any intimate or long-lasting friendships. As I have concentrated my efforts in Carcasse for the past six years and continue to do so, you may wonder why I am now back in Leon. The reason is that mysterious stranger I met almost 20 years ago living in the room at the clinic. Once again, there will more on that later in the story of my friends.

So in case you are wondering what Pere Pierre Jeanot's hand feels like when he shakes your hand, it is rough and calloused. Pere Pierre Jeanot does not yet have the luxury to possess a car to get around and uses his dirt motorbike for all transportation and hauling. He uses his bike to travel to and from Port-au-Prince, which is a very long way away. He uses his bike to lug empty five-gallon water jugs and gas cans to Jeremie and return to Leon with those containers filled to the brim. He even uses his dirt bike to haul full five-gallon water jugs and gas cans plus a passenger back to Leon.

Pere Pierre Jeanot is intimately involved with his church, clinic, school, and the community of Leon. He has stepped into his role as pastor with enthusiasm, filled with love and care for everyone. We have become brothers in a very short time. I have received many heartfelt emails from Pere Pierre Jeanot. When I first met Pere Jean Antoine, we did not have the luxury of sending emails to each other. All we had back then were letters delivered agonizingly slowly to and from Haiti.

I write the least about Pere Pierre Jeanot because I have known him the least time of all the Peres. When I talk about this new pastor with my friends back here in the United States, I describe him as "a keeper." I am sure if this book were written five years from now, most of this part of the book would be about him.

The Mysterious Stranger

"Brother" Fosy Josil

Fosy Josil is that mysterious stranger I first met living in the modified living/bedroom/kitchen room at the clinic in Leon. When I went down to check out the condition of the clinic on my second visit with my first medical team, I saw one of the rooms had been repaired and cleaned up with sparse furniture and some candles in it. Fosy Josil introduced himself as a "brother" in a missionary order that he was the head of. Fosy had seen the dire need of the people of Leon, especially its school-age children, and had started his Order to help them. In reality, I recall that I did not meet anyone else in his Order. If I did, I do not remember. All I remember is Fosy Josil.

He asked if I could help him with donations, which I did with trepidation for several years. After several years visiting with and spending quality time with Fosy (on the side) whenever I came to Haiti with our medical mission teams, he took me down the road to see a plot of land. That plot of land became an enduring monument to Fosy's dream and vision to help the children and orphans of Leon and the surrounding area.

After a short walk down the road, we stopped in front of what looked like a narrow strip of jungle that ran perpendicularly off the road. Fosy told me that it was his dream to buy the land and then build a school and orphanage, but one thing was lacking. He had no means or funds to purchase the land. Of course, he asked if I could help him purchase it. How could I say no to such a proposal? We bought the land, and Fosy cleared the land and added building by building and room by room, step by step and stone by stone and iron rebar by iron rebar and cement bag by cement bag, as additional funds became available. When sufficient infrastructure was present, Fosy then recruited a teaching staff of Professors, as they are called in Haiti. The professors had to be paid, and paid enough, so they did not leave to work for more pay somewhere else. No one would ever be as dedicated and frugal as Fosy to make his dream a reality. Over the years, I and others that share Fosy's vision have contributed to the professors' pay. Fosy has added other rooms and facilities to not only provide for education of his students, but also to provide housing, health care, and life for orphan children. The school now has 12 grades plus a kindergarten, something almost unheard of in Haiti. The school has over 550 children and over 50 orphans that receive support. These children are the poorest of the poor of Haiti. Our next plan is to build a health clinic with an attending nurse for not only the children of Fosy's school, but also for the children of Pere Pierre Jeanot's school and all the children in the Leon area. Update: We received a $25,000 grant to build the health clinic. It was almost completed when Leon was hit by Hurricane Matthew in

October 2016. The clinic was totally destroyed. We must now find new funding to rebuild the clinic.

As I stated, the clinic will be for the children of both schools in Leon, and that is the rest of Fosy's story. That is rather amazing in itself. Pere Jean Antoine had provided a safe haven for Fosy at the clinic until he was able to move into the school grounds. As far as I was able to understand the situation, Fosy had done the unthinkable as an unordained brother: he had used his organization to start a school in a Catholic Diocese without the approval of the Church. For some reason, again as far as it is my understanding, the new pastor in Leon and the Catholic Church challenged Fosy's standing as the owner of the land and the head of his school. The townspeople backed Fosy, and finally the Church backed down on its counterclaim, but not until Fosy was able to prove that, in fact, I had purchased the land for the school. Fosy now finally had a clear title to the land for his school and orphanage. Any previous relationship that Fosy had with the pastor of the church in Leon was now broken. That situation existed until recently when I found myself in Leon once again because of our inability to do a medical mission to Carcasse. I met Pere Pierre Jeanot for the first time, but this trip also gave me the opportunity to spend more personal time with Fosy than I had been able to for many years. I also set up a special clinic for the students of Pere Pierre Jeanot's and Fosy's schools.

Fosy told me about his plans to build a clinic building on the school grounds for the schoolchildren and orphans. I explained to Fosy that I might be able to obtain grant money to build the clinic since I did not have the necessary funds personally. I told him that in order to have a chance to get a grant, we had to think beyond just his school population. He had also seen how we were able to cooperate to treat children from both schools. I then talked with Pere Pierre Jeanot about the benefits of working together with Fosy for the good of all the children in Leon. He agreed to meet and talk with Fosy, and they did shortly after I came back home from Haiti. We are all now working together to make the children's health clinic a reality, and Fosy and Pere Pierre Jeanot are both my common allies and brothers.

Other Haitian Brothers and Sisters

Nurse Christiane

I met Christiane on my second trip to Haiti. Nurses who have just graduated from nursing school in Haiti (yes, there is a nursing school in Haiti!) are required to give back one year of service to the community. Christiane was living in a mountain village outside of Leon and decided to provide her services at the clinic there. The nurse I met the year before had left, and Christiane was selected to replace her. This was the beginning of a relationship that exists to this day. Christiane stayed in Leon for many years after we met. She eventually moved on and advanced her education to become an Obstetric Nurse Practitioner. Currently, she provides services to women with difficult pregnancies in Jeremie.

Christiane was a young mother with two daughters. She lived in a small village in the mountains above Leon. On one mission trip, I stayed a few extra days so I could visit with Christiane and meet her two daughters. We began walking along the riverbed and then straight up the mountain. It had recently rained (it always rains in Haiti), and it was not an easy trek for me. On the way up, I saw a quite elderly man walking down the hill with a cane. If nothing else, I was going to make it up that mountain no matter what. I did and spent a pleasant time with my limited Creole and Christiane with her less limited English visiting with her family. Now, it was time to trek back down that mountain. Halfway down, there was that elderly man now walking back up the mountain. I was thankful I was the one now going down until my foot slipped and down into the mud I went. One half of me was covered in muck. Christiane helped me up and scraped as much mud off of me as possible. Our friendship was cemented in mud.

When Christiane went back to school in Jeremie, she needed a new home there. I was able to help Christiane build a new house in Jeremie and tried to help her support her daughters the best I could. One of Christiane's daughters is now attending medical school in the Dominican Republic. Christiane continues to provide services as a Nurse Practitioner on our current medical missions and to provide care for the children of Leon until our clinic is built. On those very clear and lightless nights when you can literally see billions of stars in the Haitian sky, Christiane and I just sit quietly in the peace and quiet, undisturbed by any electronics, and say to each other and to God: Bondye Bon! (God is Good!) Update: Hurricane Matthew tore the roofs off Christiane's house and her father's house. I was able to provide the funds to Christiane to repair both houses. I definitely did not have the funds to replace the thousands of other roofs lost in Jeremie.

Pharmacist Benson

My longest continuing, ever since we met, lifelong Haitian friend is Benson (a.k.a. Robinson; a.k.a. Roberson). During my first visit to the Leon Clinic Pharmacy, I only met the nurse. I never saw anyone else running the pharmacy. That all changed the next year when I met Roberson, whom most of us non-Haitians called Robinson. Robinson, when introduced to me, said simply: You can call me Benson. Over the years, I have heard very few others call him Benson. When I mention Benson, others ask me who I am talking about.

During our first few medical missions to Leon, Benson and I were the only two pharmacists, filling up to 5,000 prescriptions during the five days. We worked from sunrise to sunset, and when necessary, using flashlights to see after the sun set. For lunch, I would run up to the rectory to get some pates and a couple of Cokes for Benson and me to eat in the pharmacy. We worked nonstop unpacking medicines, pre-packing medicines, labeling medicines, dispensing medicines, and counseling patients. Benson spoke little English, but I believe he understood more than he let on. I learned pharmacy Creole so I could function in the pharmacy on my own if I had to. In most cases, I did not have to because Benson was always there beside me. After several missions working together, Benson and I began to anticipate each other's every move. We had truly become one in the pharmacy and continue to be so.

Our relationship developed far beyond the pharmacy. When Benson's first daughter was born, he asked me to be her godfather. What an honor for me. On every mission trip to Haiti, Benson and his family and I get together. During those several years when I went to Carcasse and did not make it to Leon, Benson would show up in Carcasse to make sure that we could one more time shake hands in our special Haitian way, hug, smile at each other, and thank God for our continuing relationship.

Benson and I continue to work together, even when I am not in Haiti. Benson knows the pharmacy operations intimately. He knows where and how and when to locate hard-to-find medicines (which in Haiti are difficult to find most of the time). He has the clinic pharmacy as well-stocked as possible before each mission trip. He will make many trips from Leon to Jeremie on his dirt bike to procure medicines to haul back to Leon. It is truly amazing how much one man can load onto a dirt bike and haul over non-existent roads. Benson has even hauled me on his dirt bike over those roads at 4 AM to get me, my backpack, a duffel bag, and a carry-on bag to the bus in Jeremie. As we passed through what seemed to be some bottomless "puddles," not a splash hit me as Benson seemingly, without any effort, glided over the water. He tackled the road so that hardly a ditch, rock, and speed bump (huge in Haiti) was felt. At all times, Benson watches over me in Haiti. That is a true friend.

Mackson

I also met Mackson the first time I met Benson. Mackson's job was to police the crowd of patients and to hand out the allotted daily 120 patient admittance slips to the 200 patients that somehow fit in the clinic. Yes, the numbers do not add up, but each day we did see 200 patients. Did Mackson perform a miracle every day? I will never know. Mackson, despite working at the clinic for so many years, died from cholera during the beginning of the epidemic (Haitians are still contracting cholera to this day). He was expecting his third child, but shortly before the delivery, he became ill with cholera. He went to the hospital as he knew he should. While at the hospital, he heard that his child was to be born shortly. He left the hospital to be with his wife during the delivery, but since he was no longer being actively treated at the hospital, he succumbed to cholera instead.

I also was asked to be the godfather for Mackson's first daughter. Since Mackson did not hold one of the "better" paying positions at the clinic, I would also help fund the schooling costs for his daughter and continue to do so. A short time before Mackson died, I was in Carcasse on a medical mission and would not make it to Leon that year. Mackson made the trip with his daughter to see me in Carcasse. I kind of knew why Mackson made the trip. He wanted to make sure he got the money for his daughter, and the best way to make sure was to track me down. It was the end of a hard, long day in Carcasse when Mackson appeared to see me. I was somewhat irritated, but tried to show my best side. I assured Mackson that he would receive the promised funds. He then left to make the long trek back to Leon all in one day. That would be the last day I would ever see Mackson alive. I continue to see Mackson's wife and daughter as they now make the effort to make sure that I do not forget them. When they show up, I think: only by the grace of God.

Margo

I will just say a few words about Margo. Again, as with others, I met Margo for the first time a long time ago. When we first met, she was, and continues to be, the custodian of the clinic, making sure the clinic is swept and the garbage is picked up and disposed of. She was a very thin and frail-looking lady. She still is. When I first met Margo, she looked like an older lady, although she was probably in her 30s or maybe 40s. One never knows as Haitians normally look much older than they really are. Life is hard and life is tough, and life in Haiti sucks the life out of you. Strangely, Margo looks no older now than she did those many years ago. If you live long enough in Haiti, your body in appearance will catch up to your real age. Margo, as all staff at the clinic do, gets a small salary from the medical mission team for their services while we are there. I always slip Margo some extra funds and watch her face light up in her own special way.

Bishop Romulus

Margo was probably the least "famous" person I have ever met in Haiti, although that does not diminish her stature among men. On the other hand, Bishop Romulus is the most "famous" person that I have met in Haiti in all my years there. I do not like to meet "famous" people anywhere and have not gone out of my way in any manner to do so. The most "famous" person I ever met in the United States was Ted Williams (for those of you who do not know who Ted Williams is, check him out on the Internet under "baseball."). I said hello to Ted, wished him well, and then walked away without even asking for an autograph, which he probably would have given me for free back then when he was managing the lowly Washington Senators. Whenever I use the word "famous" and connect it with a real person, to me, the word needs to be in quotes because there has been only one famous person to ever walk the earth, Jesus Christ.

Bishop Romulus risked his life for his country and for the Haitian people. My role is not to retell his story. You can look that up, too, when you look up Ted Williams. When our medical team would come to Haiti in our initial years, we would stay overnight at the Bishop's House in Jeremie as there were many dormitory-style rooms there for visitors. We would occasionally see Bishop Romulus, especially when we were eating. Usually, the Bishop would quietly either serve us or pick up our plates when we were done. I "officially" met Bishop Romulus only once near the end of his term. He had a dream to build a new cathedral in Jeremie. The cathedral stood partially completed and is now beginning to become run down behind the Bishop's House. I recall watching laborers building the foundation and then the beginnings of the upper levels shovel by shovel and wheelbarrow by wheelbarrow. Then suddenly, the work stopped. Evidently, the Bishop had run out of funds to continue building his dream. Several members of our team met with the Bishop to wish him well and thank him for all the time and effort that he took to support our medical missions to the Grand Anse. During that time, he reflected on his past and especially the unfinished cathedral. He asked if we could somehow support him to allow his dream to be accomplished. In the end, he gave me an autographed picture. It was and still is my only autograph from a "famous" person. When I left, I knew there was nothing I could do to convince anyone to support Bishop Romulus's dream. It was one of my sadder moments in Haiti.

Pierre Louis

I first met Pierre Louis on my second medical mission to Carcasse. I never really understood Pierre's role. Evidently, he is related to Pere Verdieu in some way and goes to Carcasse on occasion to work with and help Pere Verdieu. Pierre is currently going to engineering school in Port-au-Prince. He would hang out in a work area next to the rectory where I would do paperwork when not working in the clinic. In the beginning, he would interrupt me every time I was trying to do my work. Finally, I told him to come and see me when I was not working, which he finally did. He told me about going to engineering school and his need for tuition and books. Unlike many who approached me for funds for something or the other, Pierre Louis was not overbearing in his approach. As a matter of fact, it was not until several years later that I agreed to help pay part of his tuition and book fees after he agreed to come up with his share of the costs.

Pierre Louis regularly sends me his grades and a report on how he is doing in engineering school. In 2015, he sent me a proposal to build five latrines in a village on top of the mountain near Leon where cholera had especially been a problem. I told Pierre Louis that because of all my other Haitian obligations, including his tuition and books, I did not have the funds to pay for the latrines. I asked him to work up the proposal so we could submit it for a grant along with the grant proposal for the school clinic in Leon. That we have done, and we await the results for each grant application. As with many of my Haitian friends, Pierre Louis has not only become my friend, but also my "son" and protector while I am in Haiti. Update: We received the grant to build the latrines. To finish the latrines, Pierre Louis had to deal with the ravages of Hurricane Matthew. He fought the battle and finally won. The Haitian community now has five beautiful multi-family latrines.

Honore

Whenever our teams go to Haiti, we provide a translator for each primary care provider. We do not use a translator in the pharmacy since we usually have Benson with us, and as I have, I ask those pharmacists volunteering with me to learn "Pharmacy Creole." The translators do stay with us during the whole mission, and we do socialize and eat with each other. Some translators "use" their position to try to proposition and influence members of the medical team for personal material gains. Some translators are good translators of Creole, but not so good translators of medical Creole. Some translators are good medical Creole translators but also attempt to be interpreters of patients' communication with the healthcare professionals. The best translators are excellent medical Creole translators who do not interfere in the doctor-patient dialogue. These kinds are difficult to locate. I can recall only a handful of translators who really do their job right. Honore is one of those translators.

Honore has gone out of his way and beyond his normal duties to help us with many aspects of our work in Haiti over and above the needs of the medical team. He has worked with us on water projects and works with Benson to order medical supplies when we are not in Haiti. He serves as one of the professors at Fosy's school and also teaches English lessons to the students and people of Leon. Honore serves as our main contact with our compatriots in Haiti on all necessary and needed matters. Over the years, Honore has also become one of my very special friends. During my most recent trip to Haiti, I met four "boys" from Leon who attend the local schools there. They decided they were going to teach me Creole in return for me to work with them to become better English speakers, especially in medical terminology. They sensed and know that they will not get much beyond high school in Haiti, like almost every student. Graduating high school (if a student even gets that opportunity) turns into a dead end of opportunities. Honore teaches some of the boys at his English class and serves as my on-the-ground contact for the boys. It is our goal to hopefully get these boys into higher level education, such as the new pharmacy school just starting in Haiti. After my last medical mission, I learned from Honore that one of the boy's mothers did not have enough funds to keep him in school. Honore and I contacted Pere Pierre Jeanot to tell him that I would send funds with the next medical team for the boy's tuition. The boy is now back in school. My goal is to help all of them go on to college, a near impossibility for anyone in Haiti.

They also asked me to help them understand and discern what they read in the Bible. They know that without God and His Word, they have no hope in Haiti. Update on Honore: Honore wants to come to the United States to go to college to become a pharmacist and then return to Haiti to serve his people. We began an initial process to make this happen. Since then, two major events occurred in Honore's life that have stymied us: the near death at birth of his son and Hurricane Matthew. We now have to sort this all out plus contend with the bureaucracy of trying to get a Haitian enrolled in an American school of pharmacy.

The "Boys"

Jean

Like the other three boys, I met Jean for the first time on my medical mission trip in 2015. Near the end of each of our missions, the people we serve in Haiti usually throw a thank you and bon voyage party. Fosy Josil did that for us as we were ready to leave Haiti. At the party, a young man got up. The following is a greeting that this Leon high school student, Jean, gave at a farewell party at the College Coeur de Jesus School and Orphanage during that medical mission.

Our Dear Guests,

We are very happy to welcome everyone here and to be together for making friendships and working together for the happiness and for the love of our community, but mostly for you. At first, we say thank you for coming and staying among us to become one people. We're saying thank you for the American people mostly for their help, their friendship, and so on, because this is very useful for the world, for Haiti, and for us in Leon.

Thank you again for this good work you've been doing for a long time and your helping us from 1996-2015. That's a pleasure for me to be with you in the name of the students and the orphanage and for the help you've given and other things you'll do for us. Thank you very much! We want to prove and to our best to say to you "we love you a lot." Your love is a flower in good soil in the spring. These are the reasons for our friendly gathering. As you can see, our love is for you. We'll never forget you, mostly the founders of this mission: Dr. Frank, Mrs. Pat, and other visitors.

By the way, it's a big party, a party where it is not only time to dance, but it's a time for all of us to become one nation for living and working like ants in a field. That's the best way to have a better world, a better country, and a better friendship between both of these nations. This visit represents a love token for us, a love story! That's love for mankind. We hope you're satisfied with just one word—for a word for the wise is enough.

Thank you. Have a nice one.

Before I left, Jean handed me this handwritten letter:

Dear Dr. Frank,

I'm very glad to write you this letter. I'm still thinking of you since we met together last week. I don't know how to express my gladness to you, but thank you to accept to become a good friend for me and for your advice that you gave me, mostly about: Bible, medical terms, and so on.

Today is a very nice opportunity to increase our friendship that's the union between you and me. I think love and friendship are "absence makes the heart grow fonder." The Bible talks about them a lot. Listen! I'm really sorry that I didn't write you by email, but I hope I'll write to you soon.

Having or making a friendly relation, it's not only to say: we are friends, but a true friend is someone who will catch you if you fall and lend a hand if you need it. They won't laugh at you for your flaws but love you for who you really are inside, as Jesus is.

However, the greatest of these is love. I wish that God will keep on blessing you over and over all.

I am looking forward to seeing you soon.

Peace and love!

Jean

PS: I promise you, next year, I'll be your personal translator.

I am not sure if Jean was the impetus or the consequence on my then meeting three more students. I would talk with Jean on the veranda of the church rectory. Evens was the next student to come by.

Evens

Evens also gave me a letter just before I left Haiti. It had a tone of desperation to it.

Doctor Frank,

For me, it was the worst manner for explaining to someone your problem.

And, I realize as time goes by, that life becomes more difficult and more and more sacrifice becomes harder. In spite of all, I'm still afraid to be not ashamed, but I think you'll understand my pain. Maybe you can help me.

At last, I rely on your comprehension.

Evens

When I got back home, my first email from Evens had this message:

Hi Dr. Frank,

Good to hear from you. What about your activities? I hope
everything goes well for you. Even though I know that you are
busy, I want to ask you a favor, please. Could you send to me some
good English prayer about before and after sleeping and eating? I
hope God will give you the possibility to look good in all your
activities. Right now, I am doing all that you asked me, mostly
working on my English with others. Anyway, have a good summer
holiday!

Evens

My email reply:

Dear Evens,
Good day.
How are you?
I am fine.
It is very good to hear from you.
I have missed you since I left Haiti almost four weeks ago.
I look very much for my next trip to Haiti in February 2016 to see
you, Carlos, Chayles, and Jean.
I have been receiving emails from Jean.
I asked him to greet you from me.
May you always trust in God and His free gift of salvation.
Take care, my dear friend.

Prayer After Sleeping: Thank You, Father God, for the breastplate
of righteousness, which hides my sins from you on the Day of
Judgment. Thank You, Jesus, for the helmet of salvation and for
dying on the cross and shedding your blood for my sins and thank
You, Holy Spirit, for your comfort, care, wisdom, and guidance, and
thank You, Father God, for sending Jesus to die on the cross and

shed His blood for my sins, and instilling and filling me with the Holy Spirit. Thank You, Jesus, for the shoes of the Gospel of peace, your peace beyond all understanding; thank You, Jesus, for the belt of truth for You are the way, the truth, and the life, you are the source of all truth, you are the truth, and no one can come to the Father except through You. Thank you God for the shield of faith, for I put my trust and faith in You; and thank you for the sword of the Spirit, which is above all else. Amen.

Prayer Before Sleeping: Father God, You created the Pleiades and Orion and You stride the heights of Creation, yet through Your Holy Spirit, You reveal your innermost thoughts to man. You are an awesome and mighty God. Holy, holy, holy is the LORD GOD almighty. Amen.

Prayer for Meals: Bless us oh Lord and these Thy gifts, which we are about to receive from Thy grace and bounty, through Christ, Our Lord. All praise and honor and glory are yours, Lord Jesus Christ. We ask this and pray this in the Name and Power of our Lord Jesus Christ. Amen.

Other Prayer: Thank you dear Father God, Lord Jesus Christ, and Holy Spirit for all that You do for me. Thank You for all your blessings upon me. Thank You for my family and friends. Thank you for Your free gift of salvation. You are a good and wonderful God. All praise and honor and glory are Yours now and forever. Amen.

My last email from Evens before Christmas in 2015:

Dear Dr.

How are you and your family? How are your activities?

I'm sorry that you never hear from me. The reason is because every time when I go to the internet cafe, I find no access to work. Please may you excuse me?

Tell me about the weather? Is it very cold? In Haiti it's cold a little bit.

I'm very happy that today I find the opportunity to begin by wishing you "Merry Christmas and Happy New Year!" May God bless you and your family!

Best wishes!

Evens

Chayles

Chayles was the next student to show up on the veranda. He wanted to sing several songs in English at the farewell party at Fosy's school. He asked me what the medical team would like for him to sing. I told him that most of the medical team members were women and that he should sing an American love song. He sang a song that I did not recognize, but everyone else on the team, except one member who was even older than me, did recognize. They all sang along with Chayles. He was not as outgoing as Jean and Evens but also showed an intense desire to learn English better, a desire to help me learn Creole, and a dream to go onto the University to further his education. This can be readily seen in the following letter that Chayles gave to me before I left Haiti:

Dear Mr. Franck,

I'm sorry to bother you because I write to you. I've something that at another time I will like to call you my father because I think another time I'll come to hear you.

So, I write you because every time in my mind I imagine that I have only my mother. She is very unhappy, and I will almost finish my study, which will help me to go to the University, but when I finish my study, I will not be able to go to the University. How will my life end?

So, Mr. Franck, I remember that I talk to you and you talk to me, too. So, I don't know your capacity. I don't know you inside out, but can you find the way with me, please. I beg you don't neglect to do that for me, please, and the Lord can reward you for that.

So, Mr. Franck, I think you understand me before reading (this letter).

Have a good travel.

Chayles

Chayles and I continue to email each other. This email was enlightening to me:

I have some songs to email you because I want to become a singer, too. I began to write one today for the medical mission with a speech. I'll sing the medical mission song at the party. I'll teach you in Creole. You remember I told you that you teach me, and I'll teach you.

Carlos

Carlos was the fourth student who made his way to the veranda. He was the most quiet and reclusive of all the boys and at times did not show up for his appointments. I did not receive any letter from Carlos before I left Haiti. I have yet to receive any emails since I have been back. Does that mean out of sight, out of mind? In Haiti, one never knows. I do understand that many people in Haiti do not have the luxury to send out emails at their command. It simply may be that. Before I finished writing this book, I found out from a contact in Haiti that Carlos has no way to access any means to contact me long distance. I bought a laptop that I will bring to Haiti for the four students to share. Hopefully, Carlos will get good use out of it.

Almost Forgotten

Peter Hackmann

I almost forgot Peter Hackmann. Maybe because Peter was a Black man in Haiti, but he was not Haitian. He was very much Liberian, and yet, was more Haitian than many Haitians I met. Maybe it was because I met Peter in Jeremie before I had the opportunity to meet all my future Haitian friends in Leon and Carcasse. Maybe it was because 20 years later, Peter appears to have forgotten me.

How did Peter find out about me in the beginning? He was a somewhat permanent guest of Bishop Romulus at the Eviche' de Jeremie (Bishop's House) when I was staying there. He saw me, knew why I was there, and invited me, along with a few Haitian beers, up to the rooftop of the Eviche'. That was the beginning of my quite unusual relationship with Peter Hackmann. As an example of how quite unusual our relationship would get at times, I showed up late at the Eviche' one night, and there was Peter with a bunch of glowing balls stuffed in his mouth. Peter's face was glowing from the inside like the top of a Christmas tree in the dark.

Over time, Peter would open my eyes to parts of Haiti I would never have seen otherwise. Everyone in Jeremie seemed to know Peter, or at least, it seemed like Peter knew everyone in Jeremie. He got around Jeremie on a motor scooter (not a dirt motorbike as most of those that were able to afford to ride around) because that was all he could afford. The both of us would ride all around Jeremie on the motor scooter with Peter waving or shouting to just about everyone we passed. We would stop at peoples' houses or shops. When we were not riding around Jeremie during the day, we usually were up on the rooftop at night discussing Peter's schemes. Others in Haiti seemed to have dreams while Peter seemed to have schemes, or seemingly, impossible dreams. Others seemed to have one dream; Peter always had many, and all of them needed funding to make them happen. He wanted to become a priest, a teacher (that he did accomplish), to buy land, to build and start a school, to provide medical care to poor Haitians, to go to the United States to further his education, to build houses. Peter wanted to.........................

I especially remember one day when Peter revealed his latest scheme to me. I was leaving later that day to fly back to Port-au-Prince so I could fly back to the United States. It was early in the morning, and Peter wanted to show me some land just outside of Jeremie. He assured me that we would be back in plenty of time for me to get on my plane. I would be taking my first scooter ride with Peter outside of Jeremie, but Peter assured me there was nothing to worry about. We both got on the scooter and started riding to the limits of Jeremie and then beyond. We kept riding and riding and riding until the skyline of Jeremie disappeared from view. We were now out in the country. We kept riding as Peter kept assuring me we were getting very close. I began calculating how long it had already taken us to get where we were, doubled that, and began to realize I would not make it back in time to catch my plane. Just when Peter accepted that there would not be enough time to show me the land, the scooter got a flat tire. Of course, though, Peter seemed to know everyone even in that part of Haiti, wherever it was. He said something in Creole to someone walking by, and shortly after a guy riding a dirt bike appeared. Peter gave the driver some money, and I hopped on the dirt bike and made it back to my plane just in time to board. That was not the last time I ever saw Peter, although it could well have been in my mind.

The next trip back to Haiti, I saw Peter as usual. We sat on the roof top like always. We rode around Jeremie as usual. Peter had another plan for his life. He would go to Canada, establish residency, and then be able to go to school in Vermont to fulfill his dream to finally become a priest (or, maybe with Peter, something else; I was not quite sure). He would need funds for that venture, and of course, as always, Peter sold me on his plan. I would never see Peter again in Haiti (or anywhere else, as it has turned out). Peter eventually did make it to Canada and is still there, I think! I received many emails and letters from Peter after he made it to Canada. Then, the letters stopped. The emails stopped. Well, they did not stop 100 percent. I would receive an occasional email to help Peter to go to Europe for the opportunity to do something important there, or most recently, to go to the United States and then possibly to Haiti. According to Peter, these requests from Canada would not be donations to Peter but loans that he would pay back. To date, Peter has not responded to any of my requests asking, "How are you?"

Peter, wherefore art thou?

THE Haitian People

I have met tens of thousands of Haitians. Of course, every Haitian is a different person, as certainly can be seen by "my Haitian friends." Allow me to digress and generalize before I go on. I have not met a Haitian whose life is easy, at least by the standards which we Americans live. As stated, I have not met many of the "famous" people of Haiti, so I will not make a call as to whether the Haiti President, or elected officials, or church leaders, or "important" people have it easy or not. Those whom I have met that earn nothing at all, those who earn the so-called average daily wage of one American dollar, or those that do earn more, do not have it easy. Some may have it easier than others, but no one has it easy. On top of it, Haitians are basically stuck in Haiti. I may not have it easy when I am in Haiti, but I can always come back to the United States. Plus, when I am there, even those with the least will invite me into their homes and provide for me out of what little they have. They will make sure I am fed before they are. They cannot believe that an American like me would leave his country to come to Haiti just to help them, even if it's only a few weeks at a time (or even only for one time period).

Several years ago on another one of those endless road trips in Haiti, we had to stop at some road construction (yes; there is road construction in Haiti to try to get one continuous paved road from Port-au-Prince to Jeremie. Hopefully, I might see it completed and benefit from it in my lifetime!). During a long wait, a thin woman carrying a baby and walking with a small child walked just past our stopped van and halted ahead of us as she could go no farther either. As we sat in our van, I asked the others if we could give this woman and her children a ride. Of course, they said. I invited her to sit in the van with us. After she got in, I offered her several packs of crackers that I had on me for the trip. She took them and opened one pack and ate one cracker after giving her children the other crackers. A short time later, a man and some others walked up to the van, and the woman gave them the other packs of crackers. The woman did not have to share the crackers, but she did. After a fairly long wait, the road was opened as we jockeyed ahead of a huge construction truck so we did not have to follow him all the way to Jeremie. After several miles down the long and winding road, we came into a small town where the woman lived and dropped her off. After we stopped, the huge construction truck roared by us.

We had several students from the United States in the van with us. Quite often after trips like these, the students will comment on how nasty the trip was. This time, all they could talk about was that we offered this woman and her children a ride, and she immediately turned her good fortune into good fortune for others around her.

You, the reader, may be wondering at this point in time just how many people have approached me with schemes and dreams and visions and requests for money to help obtain them. The answer is probably hundreds over time. I have committed to those in whom I truly believe. I tend to trust everyone I meet, especially in Haiti, but I am limited to the number I can help. I have probably left hundreds of thousands of American dollars in Haiti over the many years, yet I do not feel poorer. Have I ever been taken for a fool? I am sure I have. Would I do it again? I am sure I would. I have seen the enriched benefits of those I have helped and of those they have helped. Jesus was right on when He said to seek ye first the Kingdom of God and the wealth of His Righteousness, and all the things of the world shall be added onto you.

Chapter 3

Some Well Known and Not So Well Known Medical Mission Team Members

The Medical Mission Team

We started small, very small. The first official medical team member was me. The first official non-medical member was Pat Labuda. Slowly, our number grew over time until now there are or have been hundreds of team members over the years. Pat and I remain as the only original members, although there are those who joined around the five-year mark and still remain with us. Some have gone to Haiti multiple times. Some have been there once, done it once. A few have gone there, regretted ever doing so, and either gutted it out and contributed, or became an additional team burden as they bemoaned their horrible circumstances ("How could anyone do that to them?"). Two came and turned around and went right back home. There were more than a few who enthusiastically told us that this was their dream of a lifetime and would definitely go with us on the next mission and many more to come. When it came time to put the rubber to the road and purchase the airline tickets, some came up with a reason not to be able to go. Some came as students and went on to become doctors so they could serve the poor of the world in the future. Some who came started their own medical missions in other countries or in other parts of Haiti. Then there were those who came, and after their first mission, told me they would be there with me for all future missions. They never went to Haiti with me again.

The following are the stories of some of our team members.

Pat Labuda

There is no better known medical team member, inside and outside of Haiti, than Pat Labuda. Pat began going to Haiti many years before I ever stepped onto Haitian soil. Back in the 1980s, St.

Francis of Assisi Church in Derwood, Maryland became twinned with St. Paul's Church in Leon. Since that time, Pat has been to Haiti well over a hundred times. She goes multiple times per year and for weeks at a time. In the very beginning, of course, there was no medical team, and Pat went to Haiti as part of general mission trips. Pat was with me on my first "medical" mission in 1996, my first time to Haiti. Details of that trip and other medical missions will be offered in Chapter 4. From that time on, the main focus of our mission trips to Haiti has been medical, although all the general mission issues are covered while we are there.

Let me start off by saying that Pat is truly one of a kind. She has devoted her whole life to her extensive family and to the people and country of Haiti. Since she started her life work in Haiti, Pat has become immersed in all aspects of Haitian life and culture. On her own, she has become fluent in Creole. As with Peter Hackmann, Pat is well known in Haiti, but she is not limited to Jeremie or the Grand Anse province, although that is where she concentrates her efforts. Pat seems to know every necessary person in Haiti, and they know Pat. Pat can get us out of any dilemma that we will ever face in Haiti. We have never been stranded in Haiti. She is an endless bunch of energy and a ball of fire and literally never stops, although I do believe that she sleeps, as I have heard her snore. (Full disclosure: Pat and I have a pact that whatever happens in Haiti stays in Haiti. In this case, I heard Pat snore on a side trip to the Dominican Republic that we took, after being in Haiti, to visit with a girl I was sponsoring in the Dominican Republic. Therefore, I am not revealing any information about Pat snoring in Haiti. In addition, any specific newsworthy stories that appear in the rest of this book that involve Pat specifically will be reported anonymously.)

Pat is even older than I am, and I can barely keep up with her. Most mission team members, including the youngest and strongest students, cannot keep up with Pat. I have seen her, after walking up the road at the top of a long hill, on the hottest and most humid days of the year, waiting for the students still struggling up the road and still halfway down. Pat is always busy and in motion. One moment she is there, and the next moment she is gone. She always seems to be doing something else whenever it is ready for us to leave on time to be somewhere on time. It must be that she knows, like all seasoned travelers to Haiti, that you must always hurry up and wait. She also knows that without her, nothing happens anyway.

Whenever Pat and I go to Haiti, my wife tells me to make sure that Pat and I do not kill each other. She knows that Pat and I are like oil and water with our personalities. When Pat is all over the place, I am focused. When Pat is off somewhere, I am there. When Pat forgets something, I remember. When Pat is cool and calm, I am warm and excited. When Pat loses her valuables, I find them. When Pat is "x", I am "y". When Pat is "y", I am "x". What happens, though, is that like a fine marriage, we complement and compliment each other and stand up to the rest of the world. We are a team.

There is another part of Pat Labuda that I have to mention. That part is Bill Labuda, Pat's husband. Bill is the ideal husband when it comes to Pat and Haiti. She has devoted her life to Haiti along with Bill and her family. I am sure there are many times when Bill feels like he is in second place, yet he wholeheartedly, in all ways and manners, supports all that Pat does for Haiti.

That is enough about Pat for now. I will have more to say about our illustrious leader later, either specifically or anonymously (hint, hint). For now, let's move on to the next best well known member of the Haiti medical mission teams. That would be me.

Addendum: Sometimes we employ dark humor to get by the rough times in Haiti. Here is Pat's most memorable dark humor statement regarding a very old man we had just seen in the clinic: "He's got one foot in the grave, and the other on a banana peel."

Frank J. Nice

My father was Frank J. Nice, Sr. I am Frank J. Nice, Jr. My dad always used the "J." in his name, and I inherited that trait. I have a Doctorate in Public Administration and sometimes also go by Dr. Frank J. Nice. In Haiti, I am well known by:

Frank
Franck (with a short "a")
Franck, Franck (by children who want something from me)
Dr. Franck
Dr. Nice
Blan (a.k.a. Blanc, with a short "a")
Hey You, Watcha Name (by those children who do not know me by my name of Franck, Franck)

I started the medical mission twenty years ago. The details will be in the stories I have yet to spin. For the moment, I will give you just a brief synopsis of why I am so "well known," at least in this book.

Dr. Frank J. Nice has practiced as a consultant, lecturer, and author on medications and breastfeeding for 40 years. He holds a Bachelor's Degree in Pharmacy, a Master's Degree in Pharmacy Administration, Master's and Doctorate Degrees in Public Administration, and Certification in Public Health Pharmacy. He retired from the US Public Health Service after 30 years of distinguished service. Dr. Nice practiced at the NIH and served as a Project Manager at the FDA. He recently retired after 43 years of government service and is currently self-employed as a consultant and President of Nice Breastfeeding LLC (www.nicebreastfeeding.com) and President, Pacific United LLC.

Dr. Nice has published Nonprescription Drugs for the Breastfeeding Mother, 2nd Edition, The Galactogogue Recipe Book, and Recreational Drugs and Drugs Used to Treat Addicted Mothers: Impact on Pregnancy and Breastfeeding. Dr. Nice has also authored over four dozen peer-reviewed articles on the use of prescription medications, Over-the-Counter (OTC) products, and herbals during breastfeeding, in addition to articles and book chapters on the use of power, epilepsy, and work characteristics of healthcare professionals. He has organized and participated in over 50 medical missions to Haiti. Dr. Nice continues to provide consultations, lectures, and presentations to the breastfeeding community and to serve the poor of Haiti.

That is enough to be said about me. Since Pat and I are the only two medical mission team members to have been together for the past twenty years, we are by default the only two well-known members of the team. Let's move on some of our notorious, memorable (at least to me), and sometimes more illustrious team members.

Nurse Jim

I mention Nurse Jim first because he was the first person I recruited for our second medical mission team who would go to Haiti for one week. Jim and I knew each other through our church at St. Francis of Assisi. He had worked with me at the National Institutes of Health and rented out a room in my house before he got married. Of course, in putting together the first real medical team, we needed a nurse. Jim was, in a way, a captive audience because of our previous relationships, but Jim was also one of those down-to-earth, hardworking guys who readily saw the need for what we planned to do. Jim actually participated for several years until he married and started his family.

Jim's outstanding personal characteristic was his ability to sleep through anything. You cannot realize what a blessing that can be until you go to Haiti. You and your sleep have to contend with very loud, snoring team members (which we seemed to naturally attract), ringing church bells (the ones in Leon were very loud and rang each morning, on time, at 5 AM and then repeated at 5:30 AM with sharp repetition and precision—that bell ringer was the best I have ever heard), barking dogs who slept right next to you (well, they actually slept more during the hot days rather than the cooler nights), and other strange noises that go bump in the night. There will be more on this in the section on noises. Jim (and I) was fortunate to sleep in the same room as a loud snoring dentist (more to come on Dentist Jack) with a nocturnal dog nearby (more on additional Haitian dogs to come). Jim slept every night and every early morning though all of this. I basically had to drag Jim out of bed every morning to get him going. Lest you think Jim was truly blessed, he was cursed with eardrums that (although they could not hear night noises) would almost burst with pain and pressure whenever we flew the small airplane (more on the airplanes to follow) and started landing.

Dentist Jack

Dentist Jack was the first dentist ever to come on a medical mission with us to Haiti. Jack was a retired or semi-retired (I never really knew) dentist who Pat knew somehow. He wanted to see the world but at someone else's expense. Pat had to work out all kinds of deals to entice Jack to come to Haiti. She even had to accompany Jack on a trip that he wanted to make to the Dominican Republic. He was somewhat crude in his speech and mannerisms, but in the infancy of our medical missions, he was the only dentist we could find at the time. To Jack's credit, he did wonderful dental things in Haiti while he was there.

As I mentioned before, Jack shared the same room with Nurse Jim and me. Jim would fall asleep immediately (another blessing). I am one of those who lie awake forever hearing and being annoyed by every sound, even with earplugs stuffed in my ears. Jack would toss around a little bit (good) until he fell asleep (bad), which was followed by immediate snoring. Jack was also an older man with a somewhat weak bladder, so he would wake up several times a night, and his snoring would stop (good). Then, he would stumble around noisily (bad) to get to the toilet. One night, Jack also had some intestinal problems, which is fairly common for travelers in Haiti.

Well, Jack gets up and goes to the toilet—not mainly for his weak bladder, but for his intestinal issues. Once he got to the toilet, you could hear every bodily noise and sound and gastronomical perturbation and aberration possible. After what seemed like an eternity, it was over. Quiet once again reigned, but not for long. Moving away from the toilet, Jack stumbles over the dog that was, for the first time in memory, sleeping peacefully, at night no less, on the floor. Now, being stepped on brought the dog to his normal night life routine, and he started howling. Well, to be exact, both the dog and Dentist Jack started howling. It all lasted for quite some time. After finally falling asleep, it seemed like in minutes, the 5 AM bells were ringing. I remembered every excruciating moment of that night. When Jack awoke that morning, he did not remember anything, even though he lived through it. When Nurse Jim woke up, he had heard nothing. As for the dog, I do not know what he remembered.

Pharmacist Al Locke

Pharmacist Al Locke was probably the loudest snorer I ever met in my life, but that did not stop me in the least from asking him to be part of our medical mission team. I knew Al through work at the National Institutes of Health and through the PHS-1 Disaster Medical Assistance Team (DMAT). On one deployment, Al was in the non-snorers' tent, but not for long. Once he fell soundly asleep and started snoring, four DMAT members each got a corner of Al's bed with Al in it and brought it and all of Al's belongings over to the snorers' tent. For the rest of the deployment, Al never said a word. I was sure that he never knew he had been moved to another tent.

I had been working for many years as a lone pharmacist with Benson in the clinic pharmacy, but that had been mainly for only one-week missions. We were beginning to expand beyond one-week missions to two, three, and even four-week missions. Al became a stalwart pharmacist participant on our medical mission teams up to the time he died, rather unexpectedly, from cancer. After participating with me personally, Al started teaming up with a group of nurse practitioners and students from Johns Hopkins University who covered one of the other weeks of medical missions after we expanded. Al was single and liked to spend his time with the Johns Hopkins group rather than with me. I made sure that Al got his preference. Al loved the Johns Hopkins group, and they loved Al. It was a match made in heaven.

After Al died, he left a large donation to the Haiti mission in his will. Al was not only a pharmacist with the DMAT, but he was also a communications expert. The proceeds of his will were used to initiate and set up a communications system for the people of Leon. In his honor, the pharmacy at the Leon clinic is now the Al Locke Pharmacy.

The DMATs

I was a Pharmacist and Operations Officer for the PHS-1 DMAT from almost its inception. The PHS-1 DMAT was the first ever established DMAT and became the prototype for all future DMATs. Simply, a DMAT is a group of medical and support personnel designed to provide emergency medical care during a disaster or other unusual event. DMATs are designed to be a rapid-response element to supplement local medical care when needed. Standard DMAT teams provide medical care either in hospital or clinical settings (augmenting local resources that have been overtaxed) or in austere conditions such as field treatment sites established for a specific disaster response. Teams are also deployed as "standby resources" at special events such as political conventions, Presidential inaugurations, Olympics, and Special Olympics, etc. Specialty DMAT teams provide mortuary assistance, veterinary assistance, burn treatment care, surgical assistance, and mental health care.

One time, after several medical missions to Haiti, I was deployed with the PHS-1 DMAT to the Olympics in Atlanta, Georgia. I was driving down with a PHS Officer and physician, Rick Niska. To pass the time, we talked about a lot of personal and professional things. Eventually, we got around to my previous experiences in Haiti. Rick was intrigued with the possibility of participating personally, and the DMAT, as a team, in future medical missions to Haiti. We were never able to "officially" get the DMAT involved in Haiti medical missions, but we were able to get individual members to commit to go to Haiti on their personal time. Note: The PHS DMAT eventually did officially go to Haiti as part of the earthquake assistance that was provided by the United States; by the time, I was far removed from the DMAT and had retired from the US Public Health Service.

Later, on another deployment, I met another DMAT official and physician, Andy Stevermer, who also later, as an individual, participated in medical missions with me to Haiti. Andy eventually moved to the West Coast to become a regional disaster director. As part of his duties, Andy made numerous contacts with DMATs on the West Coast, including those from Oregon, Alaska, and the state of Washington. Those DMATs began using the Haiti medical missions as training opportunities as well as opportunities to serve the poorest of the poor in Haiti. To this day, these DMATs play an enormous role in the success of our medical missions. Just one example is the development of the Haiti Medical Team Treatment Guidelines. These guidelines are state-of-the-art guidelines for not only the whole medical community of Haiti, but also a prototype for use worldwide.

The Nurse Practitioner Program at the Johns Hopkins University

This is from the Johns Hopkins University website:

Dean Martha N. Hill, PhD, RN, has named assistant professor Elizabeth (Beth) Sloand, PhD, CRNP, to serve as the organizer and spokeswoman for all Johns Hopkins University School of Nursing (JHUSON) relief efforts aimed at Haiti. Beth Sloand will be coordinating JHUSON initiatives with those of the university and its other divisions. She reports that "the immediate need is for financial support to relief agencies that are already on the ground in Haiti bringing vital supplies of food, water, and shelter."

Beth Sloand is another of those treasures that God gave to our Haiti medical mission team. As with the DMAT individual treasures that the team received, we had a bonus. We received not only individuals, we also received whole medical support teams. With Beth also came the Johns Hopkins University School of Nursing. Beth was an early volunteer on our team and has remained so for well over a decade. She and her support team cover a week in Haiti in October of every year. Not only does Beth come with experienced Nurse Practitioners, but she also comes with Nurse Practitioner students, who not only participate in future Haiti medical missions, but also go on to serve the underserved of other nations.

The University of Maryland Eastern Shore School of Pharmacy (UMES SOP)

The UMES SOP is a relatively new participant as part of the Haiti medical team. The main drivers in this collaboration have been two professors at the UMES SOP, Yen Dang and Hoai-An Truong. The

UMES SOP has now participated in two medical missions and plan to be a mainstay stabilizing force after I am gone from the scene.

Here is a short summary of a recent participation by the UMES SOP in the medical mission program:

Bonjou! As we landed at Port-au-Prince airport in Haiti, we approached Haitians with a gentle greeting. It wasn't the only Creole we learned before the trip, but a one-day Creole class wasn't enough to start a casual conversation with them. Our trip began with a delay at the airport due to luggage issues that delayed our entire schedule. The bumpy roads slowed us down even more as we headed to Leon.

Our team consisted of pharmacy students, a physical therapy student, a pre-med student, and a psychology major student who graduated the day before departure. We provided clinical services and delivered presentations at two different schools. Students got opportunities to provide direct patient care in a non-traditional healthcare setting under the supervision of a pharmacist. We counseled patients on the proper use of an inhaler, triaged students for abnormal skin conditions, and distributed medications to over 900 pediatric patients. We were thankful that we were able to provide services to students who showed their gratitude by hosting a party for us on the last day. Many of us were touched and showed tears because of their warm hospitality and genuine appreciation for what we have provided.

We learned that healthcare doesn't mean the same everywhere. Not everyone gets the same healthcare that we get in the United States. We strongly feel that it is our duty to serve the underserved community to benefit their health. We felt the need to promote such a great opportunity to other students and encourage them to get involved regardless of their major or profession.

During the 7-day trip, we were able to experience the beautiful landscapes and the ocean despite the humidity and the heat that stayed with us during the entire time. We settled into a well-used 4WD van passing through mud puddles and rocks on the road. We passed clusters of children in their school uniforms and women balancing baskets on their heads. Haiti was indeed a poor country, but the elephant ear-sized leaves spreading outside of the window and countless stars on clear night skies reflect how beautiful the country is and how much we want to go back.

Dr. Dan "Coffee" Cardile

Dr. Coffee, a.k.a. Dan Cardile, has not been on the ground in Haiti as part of a medical team that I have been a member of. He has been to Haiti with his wife, Anne Cardile, who is a compassionate and caring doctor that is always volunteering to help poor people, not only in Haiti, but also in the United States. In fact, when I checked Anne's medical license, her medical practice is listed as: Volunteer. Dr. Coffee is a lawyer, yet is still a really nice guy. Dr. Coffee is the head of our Haiti Mission Committee, but that is not why he is known as Dr. Coffee.

Dr. Coffee also heads the Just Haiti Coffee (JHC) initiative at our church. JHC is a coffee cooperative in Haiti. JHC works with coffee growers and their families. It began in 2006 with one grower association in Baraderes, called Kafe Devlopmen Barade (KDB), located in the south of Haiti. It has expanded to work in communities across the country. JHC's role is to bring their high-quality, shade-grown, organically-produced Arabica coffee to North American consumers. Coffee growers in both Leon and Carcasse participate in the program.

It is just because of behind the scene supporters, such as Dr. Coffee, that the Haiti mission and medical missions exist and continue to exist. I wish I could mention every one of them. Unfortunately, I am bad at remembering names and putting names with faces, plus there have been just so many of them over the decades. I apologize for that. I have been told by those who seem to know what it takes that I am now an official citizen of Haiti. When I walk the streets of Jeremie, people now call out my name like they call out Pat's name. I am humbled by the recognition. Many think that I am actually a priest. All of this tells me is that I would not have been able to do what I have done over the decades without the support of these hundreds (could it now even be thousands?) unrecognized supporters, both in and outside of Haiti. God has used all of us mightily and for His purpose. Bondye Bon! Update: As with just about everything else in our service areas, Hurricane Matthew wiped out the coffee crops in both Leon and Carcasse. The trees were stripped from the ground. It will now be another four to five years before newly planted coffee trees will again begin to produce beans.

Dr. Nice meets one of his fans at the orphanage on the last day in Leon.

Chapter 4

Evolution and Revolution of the Medical Mission Team

Overview

All medications and supplies are purchased with donations and stored in luggage that is checked in at the airport. Each team member pays for all of his/her expenses out of pocket. Additionally, each individual lives a minimalistic lifestyle out of his/her carry-on luggage in Haiti, which is used to carry personal items.

The medical teams treat approximately 6,000 patients and fill more than 20,000 prescriptions yearly. On each mission, several lives are saved by the teams' primary medical interventions. By concentrating our efforts at the two clinics in Leon and Carcasse (although we also run pilot clinics to help other volunteer organizations establish their own missions), we have been able to create and witness substantial changes in healthcare in Haiti.

Over the past 20 years, we have established medical records systems, referral processes, a club foot program, a free clinic for patients to receive medical care and medications while we are not there, Haitian checking accounts to purchase medications while in Haiti, medical guidelines to treat all medical conditions seen in Haiti, pharmacy Creole instruction sheets for pharmacy staff, and collaborative efforts with Haitian foundations and Cuban healthcare professionals at nearby hospitals. Additionally, the teams have been involved in installing an indoor sink and toilet and solar panels for onsite electricity at the Leon clinic. Outside of direct medical care, we have built the first 12-grade schools in the region, provided clean water resources, established food programs, and renovated the existing medical clinics. In those years that we have provided our services, the region's citizens now receive healthcare and education with dignity and respect.

The Beginning

In the beginning in 1996, the medical mission team consisted of one pharmacist – me. I was not meant to be a medical mission team all by myself, but you have to start somewhere.

Our first trip to Haiti was not meant to be a medical mission in any sense of the word. St. Francis of Assisi Church had a notice on its bulletin board asking if any members would like to go on a one-week visit to our sister church in Leon. I had never done anything like this in my life, let alone go to a mysterious country like Haiti. I was at a point in my career where I was wondering what being a pharmacist was really about and just what I was contributing to society with my God-given talents. I decided that I had nothing to lose and signed up to go. I was going as a church member who also happened to be a pharmacist. I heard that the church had a clinic, so I would do the nominal pharmacy thing to do: collect drug samples to take to the clinic. Back in those days, the Food and Drug Administration had not yet cracked down on what was perceived to be the use of samples to influence physicians and pharmacists to use certain products over others. So, I rounded up two duffel bags of samples. Back then, you could check in two free 75-pound pieces of luggage (it is now only one free 50-pound check in, and only on international flights). Whatever we need to live on during our time in Haiti, we had to fit into our carry ons (that is still true to this day).

With me on the trip to Haiti were Pastor Don Worch from our church; the aforementioned Pat Labuda; Bernie, our social needs director; and Mike, our youth minister. We departed on a February day in 1996. As we flew over the airport in Port-au-Prince, the closest scene it reminded me was the Arizona desert. In those days, when we overnighted in Port-au-Prince, we stayed at a guest house called Solidarity House. It was named in support of those brave Haitians who had given their lives opposing the ruling dictatorship (Papa Doc and then Baby Doc). Before we flew to Leon, we toured sights in Port-au-Prince where opponents of the regime were killed in one way or the other. It was uneasy times in Haiti then, in more ways than one. It was somewhat of a relief to board the small plane to Jeremie from where we drove on to Leon.

A strong hurricane had hit Haiti at the end of the year before. Leon was along the Riviere Voldrogue. During that hurricane, the one and only bridge to Leon across the river had been washed downstream. When we arrived, a temporary foot bridge was being constructed where the destroyed bridge once stood. We prepared to walk across the slightly swollen river when one of the workers drove over in the pay loader that was being used to construct the foot bridge. He lowered the bucket, and we all crawled in. We could not have asked for a grander entrance to the road into Leon. We then walked the rest of the way to the rectory to meet Pere Jean Antoine for the first time. The weather in the mountains and jungle at that time of the year was quite rainy and fairly cool and actually very pleasant for Haiti.

On our walk up to the rectory, we passed the clinic building. From the outside, on a dreary day, it did not look too bad. I was amazed at how large it was. The nurse was not in that day, so we waited until the next day to visit the clinic and pharmacy, which I was informed actually existed. The next day, we walked down with the two duffel bags. I was so excited about the "big" contribution I would be making to the pharmacy stock, kind of rounding out the current supply to make it last even longer. Upon entering the clinic hallway, I was taken aback by how it was even drearier than the outdoors. There was no lighting, it was damp and dank, and leaking water was just about everywhere. My hopes for what I would see in the pharmacy began to dim also. The nurse unlocked and opened the door, and I went in. It was small, but it looked huge because it was so bare. I did not even count more than a dozen medication bottles in the whole place. I felt despair about the next step I was about to take. I began to dump out and sort out the contents of the two duffel bags. I would not be rounding out any stock by any means. In fact, I would be trying to fill huge holes. We carefully and neatly spread the contents around the pharmacy wall shelves. When we were done, it was as if we had spit in the ocean. It was at that exact moment that I knew this was not acceptable and something had to be done. I had to come back next year and would be back with a medical mission team. I knew from my DMAT pharmacy and operations experience that I could make it happen; I just was not sure how I would make it happen. Having made it to Haiti safely, I knew I could trust God to make it happen, and over the years, God came through big time.

The Second Year

I had a year to make my plan a reality. Pat would take care of the in-Haiti logistics, but otherwise, it was up to me to make it happen on my own. I had to find sources of drugs and medical supplies (I knew that just a couple duffel bags of samples would not do it), I had to pick them up in my pickup truck or have them delivered to my house (which for many years would become the Haiti Medical Mission Warehouse), sort upon arrival, repackage into more condensed units to cut down on sheer volume, put into bags, boxes, chests, or whatever would hold 75 pounds, and then transport two of them to each member of the medical team. That was merely the hard, physical, backbreaking work. I also had to find healthcare volunteers to go to Haiti and then help them make all the necessary arrangements to get there.

During that time period, the PHS-1 DMAT was reorganizing its warehouse and replacing its supplies and wooden medical chests with a newer cache. Basically, all I had to do was drive my pickup truck out to the warehouse and load it up. That I did for what seemed like hundreds of times. The basement of my house slowly began to fill up and look like the adjunct DMAT warehouse. There were approximately 50 old wooden medical chests stacked and medical equipment and supplies in every nook and cranny. At that time, I heard about Dr. Gil Irwin, whose organization, Medical Missionaries, was in Manassas, Virginia. Gil had several huge warehouses on some donated property near Manassas and could supply you with pieces of equipment from small medical units up to huge pieces of medical machinery. When not seeing his own patients in his practice, Gil would drive up and down the East Coast hauling his trailer behind him collecting every medical artifact imaginable. He also has this long-standing relationship with the Catholic Medical Mission Board (CMMB) to obtain what seemed like unlimited donations of drugs. That arrangement is both good and bad. As was stated, the pipeline provided unlimited, and free of charge, drug donations. That was good. That was also bad in a way. Gil would have so much "free" stuff (a lot with expirations dates of less than a year, making the drugs useful for only one or two mission trips). In addition, CMMB would supply only what the drug companies had in excess with short expiration dates for that year. The specific drugs changed every year, but the total amounts did not.

I would drive down to Manassas to pick up my Haiti drugs, as it was cheaper than having Gil mail them to me. I would send Gil a list of drugs I needed and how much of each drug. When I arrived at the back door of Gil's office, Gil would open the door holding my list in his hand. There would be boxes already stacked up, plus other boxes in a trailer that Gil kept out back. I would start loading up my truck as Gil would convince me to take even more supplies or point to the trailer and tell me to take certain boxes out of it. After a while, I would be loaded up. Once at home, I lugged everything down to the basement, which fortunately had a walk out at the back of the house. I tried driving my pickup truck directly to the walkout to make it easier, but the wheels began to sink into the ground. Over the years, I made thousands of walking trips back and forth to that walkout pushing a hand truck, ever so slowly, across and into the now muddy trail in the grass.

Even with the medical supplies from the DMAT and the drugs from Gil, there was always a need to fill in other missing items. Other people who were involved in medical missions told me about Interchurch Medical Assistance (IMA) and MAP International. I could order medical supplies and drugs for foreign medical missions at steep discounts. IMA was located in New Windsor, Maryland, a drivable distance from my house. At that time, IMA had a very large, loaded warehouse. I was able to find almost everything else that I needed to take to Haiti. Once again, I would drive up to New Windsor multiple times to load up my pickup truck. A benefit of working with IMA was that I was able to form a very close personal, professional, and spiritual relationship with just about everyone who worked there. We would always go out for lunch when I picked up the supplies and many other times when I was not. From what I can tell, IMA is no longer in the main business of providing medical supplies for Haiti, and the last person that I met back then has finally retired. I will never forget my experiences and relationships with IMA. MAP is located in Tennessee. From MAP, I was able to obtain special medical mission kits or packs that served our initial limited teams very well with good basic medicines for a mission in Haiti.

I was fairly easily able to put together an initial medical team for Haiti from members of the St. Francis Church. Nurse Jim was my first volunteer. We would go to Haiti even if it were only Jim and I. Of course, Pat would go with us and be our translator. There were now three of us. We then found a doctor and were really good to go. What awaited us on our fist medical mission to Leon was indeed one of those times beyond belief.

We had made arrangements with Pere Jean Antoine to have the clinic ready and the patients ready and the clinic staff ready for the visit of the first medical team ever to that region of Haiti. They were the only arrangements made. When we arrived the first day of the week for the clinic, the clinic building was not the peaceful, quiet, dreary building during my last visit. The building was surrounded by hundreds (it sounded like a thousand) of patients. They had been told only that a medical mission team was coming for the week and to show up for care. Word had spread across the Grand Anse on both sides of the river into the jungle and up and over into the mountains and valleys. We worked our way to the front stairs of the clinic where women were frying a variety of food, with the rising smoke enveloping all who passed. After wedging our way into the clinic, we still found people everywhere. With help from the clinic staff, we were able to get at least breathing room and several places to set up practice. I found my way to the pharmacy and thankfully found Benson. With amazing speed and precision, Benson filled the pharmacy shelves. Fortunately, he had small plastic bags to which we could attach small sticky labels with the drugs' directions for use. After that, the first thing we needed to locate were several sheets to drape on the crude exam tables. The same sheet would remain on each table for the whole week. After that, we were in business for the week! What a business and learning experience it was.

Of course, everyone then wanted to be seen first, and why not? This might be their once in a lifetime opportunity to see a doctor and to get medicines. Starting then and throughout the day, there was a lot of pushing, shoving, screaming (women), shouting (men), and apparent fighting. Mackson and his clinic staff, along with Benson's help, did all they could to contain and triage the group to be seen and treated. At that time, we did not have an initial triage scheme for seeing patients, and we did not have medical records or prescription pads to write histories, diagnoses, treatment plans, or the prescriptions. All we had were scraps of paper that we handed to each patient to bring to the pharmacy for medications and final instructions. We would see approximately 200 or more patients each day until it got so dark that we could not see anymore. Then, we would tell all those left outside to come back tomorrow, and that they did in full force again.

We repeated the day before scene again with the same results as it got dark again. It didn't matter if they had nowhere to stay overnight; they would just have to figure that out. By the next day, Mackson, maybe it was the Pastor, maybe it was ourselves, figured out a system to give out numbers, from one to 120, and those were the patients that would be seen that day and in that order. It worked somewhat better with the main commotion being who would get these numbers of privilege and who could figure out a way to sneak in. Some would actually forge our doctors' names on pieces of paper that they handed to us in the pharmacy for drugs, usually Tylenol or elastic bandages, good sellers on market day. The system was certainly not ideal as we saw many more than 120 patients once again until dark. The fourth day was probably our best as everyone started getting used to the numbering system. The fifth day rivaled the first day. Patients still waiting since the beginning of the week were beginning to panic that they might not be seen at all. We also knew that at the end of the week, we were about to or had already run out of a lot of our medications and supplies. We made do with what we had left. In the end, all we had left to give out were those two special and precious items, Tylenol and elastic bandages. As we saw the last of the patients now after dark and using flashlights, we had seen the last and had essentially cleaned out our supply room and pharmacy and cleared off the shelves.

Exhausted, and still alive, we had survived with many lessons learned for our next medical mission:

1. Have the Haitian pastor or the local health committee triage all potential patients before our medical mission teams would arrive in Haiti.
2. See the sickest patients or the patients who have travelled the furthest first (for the week and for each day).

3. Use a numbering system that could not be compromised by outsiders (yes; insiders could compromise the system and did for "friends").
4. Assign clinic staff for crowd control.
5. Set up a medical records system for patient identification and ongoing care.
6. Have the pastor show up periodically at the clinic site.
7. More than a one-week mission was needed to see to the overwhelming patient population.

Transitioning

Many changes were made over the initial years. We were able to incorporate the in-Haiti clinic changes as recommended above. Dramatic improvements were made to the clinic infrastructure due to the generosity of the members of St. Francis of Assisi Church. Many things were changed by necessity back home also, for me, and for the medical teams.

When all we needed was one medical mission team for one week each year, it was not too difficult to recruit the needed team members, especially from among the members of St. Francis of Assisi Church. Eventually, we expanded to four and even five medical teams, with each team covering one week. Trying to coordinate that many teams for one medical mission became quite difficult. Also, we were only providing medical services to Haiti once a year around the month of February. We then moved to two medical mission trips per year with each mission providing teams for two to three weeks during January and June of each year. We added another medical mission in October of each year. Later on, we decided to partner with St. Mary's Church of Barnesville, Maryland to conduct a yearly October medical mission to its twinned church in Carcasse, Haiti. The medical mission schedule became three times a year, usually two medical teams to cover two weeks each time in January, June, and October. Covering that many medical teams with the healthcare members of St. Francis of Assisi Church and the smaller-sized St. Mary's Church was not possible. Thus, we extended our recruitment area outside of our churches to the DMATs, Johns Hopkins, the National Institutes of Health, The Food and Drug Administration, and anywhere else that we had the contacts.

The good result was that we have been able to sustain our medical mission teams with dedicated, outstanding, devoted, competent, compassionate, and devoted individuals and organizations. The sad truth and result has been an almost lack of personal and professional commitment from the church members of our two sponsoring churches to provide or even recruit on-the-ground healthcare professionals. To my utter frustration and sometimes embarrassment, I am the only church member pharmacist who has actually gone to Haiti on medical missions. That is not to say that I am not truly appreciative of the at-home assistance and help we have received from several church member pharmacists at St. Francis of Assisi Church. After ten or several years of doing it all when it came to medical supplies and drugs, my body, my truck, and my house could take it no more. Several pharmacists have stepped in over the later years to help me with those chores and to devise better systems and ways to procure and deliver the supplies to Haiti. We now purchase as many supplies within Haiti as possible (not always possible as medicines are continually in short supply or out of stock in Haiti). In addition, the church members of both churches have been extremely generous in providing financial support. Yet, it is difficult to even get church members to go to Haiti as lay people let alone as healthcare professionals. It is my hope and desire that one of these days, God will use our church members to do what those outside of our churches are already doing. Christians, Protestants, Hindus, Muslims, Buddhists, atheists, and agnostics have volunteered to our medical mission teams. Should not also my fellow Catholic Christian church members be doing the same in droves?

Where We Stand Now

After the 10 to 15 years' timeline of our medical mission history, especially with the expert input from DMATs and Johns Hopkins groups, in my mind, the healthcare clinics that we support seem to be running on automatic, at least compared to where we started. As what happens with any start-up organizations, the one who started the organization tends to get left behind as his successors possess the necessary abilities and skills to maintain the organization and come up with better ideas and plans to keep it going. That certainly has been the case with the clinic in Leon and is starting to become the case with the Carcasse clinic. I now stand in awe when I go to Haiti for medical missions and watch all the good stuff that is going on around me and think that this all started with me. I am truly humbled. I know that it was only possible because of how God used me to accomplish this purpose of His in Haiti.

I feel desire to move on and beyond this as my life so quickly passes before me, especially in my seventh decade on earth. That is why I am now collaborating with the University of Maryland Eastern Shore School Of Pharmacy and the Notre Dame University Baltimore School of Pharmacy to make the medical mission in Carcasse a sustainable one for when I am long gone. That is why I am now drawn back to Fosy's school in Leon to help him build a health clinic for the children and orphans of Leon. That is why I am continually drawn to make Fosy's school a legacy for him. That is why I continually seek out other ways to help the people of Haiti. That is why I seek out people all over the world to make a positive impact in Haiti. I have learned many lessons in Haiti. Below are some of them. To me, number seven (7) has been the most important.

Lessons Learned

1. **Flexibility and adaptability:** Haiti is not the United States. It has little or no infrastructure – only several hundred miles

of paved roads (if not flying to Jeremie, a 180 mile drive will take 12 hours from Port-au-Prince) and no running water, inside toilets, and electricity. One must be flexible and able to adapt to these conditions immediately.

2. **Resourcefulness**: With no infrastructure, one must be able to utilize what little is available (e.g., sunlight, flashlights, "outdoor toilet facilities," mosquito repellent, ear plugs, boiled water, beans and rice). Haitian lay people can be taught to extract teeth and treat club feet. The church pastor can be trained to triage, refer, and/or treat patients at the free clinics that we have established. Pastors are the governing infrastructure. They feed, educate, transport, counsel, and secure medical treatment for the Haitian citizens.

3. **Functioning in an austere environment:** Haiti is the poorest country in the Western Hemisphere and in the world. Carcasse is an isolated seaside village in one of the poorest parts of Haiti. It is a mosquito and bed bug infested area with very high temperatures and humidity. There is no infrastructure outside of the local church. Anyone participating in such a mission must be aware of these conditions and be capable to continue functioning.

4. **Controlling emotions:** The poverty existing in Haiti is beyond imagination. People die from medical conditions that would be easily treatable in developed countries. You will witness diseases and disorders that you have never observed and on a scale that you have never seen. It is important that volunteers understand that while it is not possible to save everyone's life, we can still make a difference in the community by saving as many lives as we can.

5. **Doing a lot with very little:** Each mission is funded with approximately $10,000. These funds provide for all of the medications, supplies, all referrals (referral fees include transportation of the patients), hiring of translators for each primary care provider (pharmacists do not use translators and communicate with patients utilizing pharmacy Creole and a Haitian pharmacy technician), and paying Haitian healthcare providers (doctor, pharmacy technician, lab technician, and two nurses) for their services.

6. **Reverse triage:** Funds and time are extremely limited. We attempt to treat as many patients as we can with the funds that we have. In many cases, we are able to provide care to patients with treatable conditions who otherwise would live in misery until the condition improved or the patient died. We have also provided comfort for the worst medical cases. However, sometimes despite our efforts, death does happen in front of our eyes. It is not uncommon to see pregnant mothers with cerebral malaria dying along with their babies.

7. **One person can make a difference:** One medical team member can save a patient's life or provide hope to a patient in a seemingly hopeless situation.

Regardless of what medical condition an individual has, when a Haitian patient looks into your face, it is like their eyes are saying to you, "You are my only hope. If you do not help me, no one will." You look back into that person's eyes and you know that you can and do make a difference in his or her life.

Chapter 5

Getting Around In Haiti

Trains, Feet, Bicycles, Scooters, Burros, Taxis, Tap-Taps, Cars, Trucks, Vans, Buses, Boats, Planes, and Ways You Would Not Even Think

Haiti offers many and varied ways of getting around the country.

Trains

Between 1876 and about the 1970s, Haiti had various tramways and railways. A tram network operated in the capital, Port-au-Prince, between 1897 and 1932. Two railway lines, Port-au-Prince - Léogâne and Port-au-Prince - Manneville, along with some industrial lines, constituted the Haitian national rail network. Trains currently are not an option anywhere in Haiti.

Recently, I returned from a trip to China. As I rode on the high speed train in China from Beijing to Hangzhou, a distance of over 800 miles, I reflected on the four and a half hours that the train trip would take. I thought about the 180-mile trip from Port-au-Prince to Carcasse that can take up to 12 hours or more. I also was fortunate to take a cross-country trip by train from Washington, DC to the West Coast and back. I was not as impressed by the 40 miles per hour that our train labored over the tracks as I was by what the train tracks went over, around, under, and through. It is a fact that trains can haul more people and a lot more cargo and goods than any other form of transportation. What if Haiti had only one train track across the country? What if the tracks had been laid back in those times where men could do wonders with not much machinery and not much money? What if the United States, during one of its occupations of Haiti, had built a railroad, if only for its own means? In Haiti, there are a lot of "what ifs.

Feet

Most people who wish to move from one place to another in Haiti use their feet. There is no other option. It is the only option if the distance is just across the street, whether it is to get across town, or to walk over or around a mountain or river to get to a medical clinic. I can testify to Haitian grandmothers walking from a distant town overnight to get to one of our clinics. One time, we ran out of medicine for the grandchild of one of those grandmothers. The grandmother had walked all the way down the mountain from her village. We told the grandmother that we would have the medicine the next day and would deliver it to her village. She apparently only heard that we would have the medication the next day. After all, who would deliver medicine to a grandmother up in the mountains? The next day, shortly after the medicine had been sent to the village, the grandmother showed up at the pharmacy. When we told her what had happened, she turned around to begin her long walk back up the mountain to get the medicine that had already been delivered.

Bicycles

Unlike the ubiquitous bicycles in China, I have seen only a handful of bicycles in Haiti. It must be the rough and mountainous terrain.

Scooters

As with bicycles, I have seen few scooters in Haiti. I think I know why. One of my friends was riding a scooter. I asked if it had a 49 cc engine like the one I have in the United States. It was actually about three times larger. I was impressed. Another Haitian friend looked at the scooter and called it a "sissy" bike. I have seen only one child's scooter in Haiti. These are the ones that are foot propelled.

Burros

Very few Haitians own burros. I usually see some whenever I go to Haiti, mostly tied next to the road to forage. The only time I see them in town is on market day as they are loaded with the market goods. Rarely do I see them ridden. So, like the option of a train to ride in Haiti, the burro option is almost as rare. By the way, we hear so much about how badly Haitians treat their burros, but I never really saw that. In fact, to me, most burros looked better off than most of their skinny farm animal counterparts.

Taxis

Taxis in Haiti are not taxis. Motor dirt bikes are taxis. If you were poor in Haiti, you walked; if you are a level above, you can afford to ride or even own a dirt bike. Most dirt bikes are owned and operated by young men. Unlike in China, you rarely see a woman driving a dirt bike. Dirt bikes are fairly common in both the city and in the countryside. Dirt bikes haul people, and they haul cargo, separately and together. They can haul a lot of people and a lot of cargo, separately and/or together. You will see a whole family of father, mother, and several children riding a dirt bike. You will see, as with Pere Pierre Jeanot, two people plus two five-gallon water jugs, plus a gasoline can being transported on a dirt bike. You will see construction materials and equipment delicately balanced upon a dirt bike. You will see objects many times the length of the dirt bike perched in the air. There is a word of warning for all naïve medical missionaries walking upon the road when a dirt bike approaches: get out of the way as far off the side of the road as you can because, even then, you will barely avoid being hit. There is not even any respect shown for aged pedestrians. It seems sometimes that the older you are, the better and more fun you are as a target. By the way, in case you thought about what to do when it rains, think banana tree leaf or plastic bag held over your head. In any case, considering all that can be done upon a motor dirt bike, they have earned the title of "taxi."

Tap-Taps

When you think of the American concept of taxis, now you can think tap-taps in Haiti. These are not the cars you see in our country or other countries. They are small pickup trucks with an open back truck bed with high rails around the box of the truck. When someone wants to board, they tap on the tap-tap. Hopefully, the tap-tap stops so you can jump in or someone pulls you in or on. One more person seems to always fit into or onto a tap-tap, no matter how overloaded it is. You can get off whenever you are ready. I have ridden a tap-tap only a few times, not necessarily because foreigners are warned not to, but being more intimidated by just how this all works. The observation most amazing to me is how uncommon it is that I see one of these contraptions broken down.

Cars

In reality, one sees very few cars in Haiti. Your typical car (well, also your typical pickup truck) would not stand the beating it takes in Haiti. You see most cars around the airports being used as we use taxis in the United States. Occasionally, you will spot a car on a Haitian road, mainly in a large city. Most cars nowadays in Haiti are SUVs. If I were writing about cars in the United States, I could write a whole book on just this topic. As for this book, it is time to move on to trucks.

Trucks

Trucks are fascinating in Haiti, at least to me. You can see small pickup trucks (a.k.a. tap-taps), large pickup trucks (American: hardly any at all; Japanese: everywhere), garbage trucks (I have seen two so far in 20 years), trucks for hauling many people plus animals and goods, called buses in Haiti since people are also aboard, gasoline trucks and huge construction trucks (impressive for some reason in Haiti, especially being driven around the city), and hand-pulled trucks (carts). Whether the trucks are hand-pulled or are diesel-powered, they are all loaded by hand (I am not so sure about the gasoline trucks, but in Haiti, you cannot know). Do you know how hard it is to load a dump truck by hand, and do you know what is usually loaded into dump trucks? Boulders, cement, sand, gravel, huge sacks of rice and charcoal. My father drove a big coal dump truck, and he would take me along with him. It was so cool to sit high up there in this huge machine towering above every other small vehicle on the road. I felt a certain truck-like privilege. I believe the Haitian truck drivers have this same sense of being above it all, at least while they are in their trucks and moving. At the same time, there is nothing sadder for a trucker to see than his truck broken down on the side of the road with a huge flat tire or a broken axle.

Vans

Once again, there can be a variety of what is considered a van in Haiti. When I first went to Haiti, most vans you saw were fairly broken down, even the ones that we were usually transported in from and to the airport. Seats were semi-attached, it was hot and sweaty inside, and you often wondered if the van would make it up the next hill without you all having to get outside and push it up. Most vans were the 12 passenger type vans, although you could always squeeze in a few more if necessary. To save space, all luggage was tied on top and hopefully, well secured. Just to be sure, one passenger was assigned to peer out the back window (if one was there) to watch for falling suitcases or flying duffel bags). Yes, you would see some nice vans around, but they were usually occupied by some people looking very official or were United Nations vans patrolling mainly to show how nice their vans looked with the big UN sign painted on them.

The vans that you see in Haiti now are vastly improved. Since the local airline in Haiti is no longer flying, those who could afford to fly now must make intercity van reservations to travel around the country. Thus, the vans now can hold up to 30 people in air conditioned (when it works) comfort while sitting in easy seats (unless you are 6 feet, 2 inches tall like me while holding my travel bag on my lap) with seat belts and arm rests.

Buses

Buses are much like the large trucks in Haiti; in fact, many are trucks. Buses mainly transport people, but just like anywhere else, they can also haul cargo. In Haiti, they can also serve as animal carriers. I have ridden several of the big buses in Haiti (the ones that look similar in size to school buses in the United States), but only when they were chartered specifically for our medical teams. I never had the opportunity to ride one of those buses or truck buses loaded with people inside and out, swaying all over the mountain roads on their lumbering journey between Jeremie and Port-au-Prince or the other way around. For anyone to make the journey between distant cities in Haiti, you are pretty much limited to riding these behemoths because of cost and availability on a doable schedule. By the way, yes, these are the buses that are brightly painted with many religious phrases and words like Glory to God and Jesus. As an aside, you will also see a variety of old school buses from the United States. Uncannily, you can usually figure exactly where in the United States they came from down to the school district, such as the Pascagoula School District of Mississippi, or the First Christian Church of Anytown, USA.

Boats

Yes, I have been transported in a boat in Haiti, just not one of those big ferries that ply the coasts. We have had medical supplies transported by ferry from Port-au-Prince to Jeremie at times, but not me. As far as I know, Pat has been the only medical team member to do that so far. Then again, Pat will do anything in Haiti to get where she needs to go. I rode in a small boat, defined as a large row boat with a big motor on the back, one time from Carcasse to the next town because the roads were impassible due to a heavy rain. I would have to say that it was one of my more pleasant trips in Haiti.

There was enough fresh cool air, and the trip was short enough to stave off any motion sickness, and it was much faster than doing it by truck. To keep things in perspective, travelling by ferry in Haiti can be very dangerous. Ferries have sunk with large death tolls. The town of Leon lost citizens, including mothers and fathers, after one of these sinkings. We know their orphans.

Planes/Airports

The planes that fly within Haiti, when they do fly, are quite unusual, as are the airports in Port-au-Prince and in Jeremie, the only two places I have flown to or from in Haiti. First of all though, just what kind of planes fly to Haiti from the United States? I imagined flying to Haiti in some kind of small, commuter type plane. I was surprised when I boarded a double-decker plane in Miami for Haiti, and it was full. Half the plane seemed to be filled by Haitians and the other half by missionary groups. When I had decided to go to Haiti for the first time, several friends told me that a place like Haiti was too dangerous to visit. When I saw so many missionaries on the plane and so many teenagers as part of those teams, and when I realized the size of the plane we were in, any fears that I had disappeared. When landing at the airport in Port-au-Prince, I noticed several fire engines at the far end of the runway. I learned soon after that one of those planes that flew from Jeremie to Port-au-Prince had crashed and that all occupants were killed. To add to that, we also were told of another plane that had crashed taking off from the Jeremie airport. The plane came down at the end of the runway. Everyone on the plane was injured, including the pilot, who helped pull the last passenger off the plane before it caught fire and burned. The plane had been overloaded with cargo and luggage.

The airport in Port-au-Prince is actually two airports with one long runway that extends from the large airport that we landed at to the small airport where the small plane had crashed. Although there is only one runway, there are two terminals. If you land at the large airport and need to take a plane that flies within Haiti, you must leave the airport, take a taxi for one mile down the road, and enter the small terminal to continue your flight. Taxis in the beginning were five American dollars for that one mile trip; now, they are ten American dollars—not a bad deal for the taxi drivers. Once, I did walk between the airport terminals and met many "friends" who offered to help me with my luggage, so walking ends up costing the same.

When we continue on a plane in Haiti, we fly on a 12- to 18-seater plane built in Russia, operated by a Dominican airline company, and flown by South American pilots. Everyone is weighed and everyone's luggage is weighed to make sure that the plane is not overloaded. Because of this requirement, we often cannot get all of our medical supplies on the plane with us and must find other ways to transport the supplies, such as sending them on the ferry. The airport at Jeremie consists of a gravel dirt runway where someone is in charge of blowing a whistle when the plane is arriving to get any stray cows and children off the runway.

The pilots fly by sight and do not fly in any bad weather. As you land, you approach the runway above a high cliff off of the water. Of all modes of travel in Haiti, I probably felt safest on these airplanes. I would always sit, if possible, right behind the pilot and copilot in the open cockpit. The pilots always look confident. They would rev up the engine at full throttle with the brakes on and check all the instruments. The copilot would confidently put his right arm and elbow on the frame of his open cockpit window before taking off and then close the window as we got up into the air. Being able to fly from Port-au-Prince saves ten hours or more of ground travel and the accompanying heat and sweat while being jammed into a truck with two others on a seat built for two plus the gear shift and accompanied by much nausea and vomiting. The trip from between Port-au-Prince and Jeremie takes only 45 to 50 minutes.

Before I conclude my comments on planes, I want to mention two other airlines in Haiti. The first one was a startup Haitian airline that tried to compete with the American and Canadian airlines for international business. Air D'Ayiti was a short-lived airline run by Haiti, which was operational between 1997 and 1999. It operated scheduled and charter flights within the Caribbean and to Miami in the United States. I actually saw one of their planes at the airport in Port-au-Prince (it always seemed to be the same plane each time I saw it) and was impressed at the venture to compete with the then current airlines that could basically charge whatever they wanted to get you in and out of Haiti. Unfortunately, due to lack of funds, and more importantly, a lack of safety and maintenance, the airline went out of business. I was surprised to see that it lasted as long as three years. I never got the chance to fly on Air D'Ayiti.

The other airline is operated by Mission Aviation Fellowship (MAF). MAF states that there is a direct correlation between living in isolation and chronic poverty. Because many people living in remote places have never heard the Gospel, MAF believes that everyone—even the isolated—deserves a chance to experience the love of Jesus Christ. Because when people in isolation have a medical emergency and often cannot get the help they need, MAF uses aviation, technology, and training because these are the only ways to reach isolated people with Christ's love. In times of need, DMAT volunteers have been able to charter MAF Planes to get to the mission field in Haiti. We are deeply appreciative of what our fellow Christians are doing in Haiti.

Ways You Would Not Even Think

I stated that most Haitians travel by foot. Some Haitians do not even have that luxury. We see them often at our clinics. For some reason, club foot seems to be far more common in Haiti than the rest of the world. We would see many adults who were born with club feet. We would see many children born with club feet. There was not much we could do for the adults except help them get around better, if possible. There was one man who figured out a way to move around that no one could improve. He used a short stick in one hand while balancing himself with his other hand and somehow dragging his club feet along. Seamlessly, he could move faster in his environment than I could by walking. He seemed to flash by. The ideal, of course, is to help those born with club feet walk as normally as possible. Because of the cost to refer these children to club feet programs, we initiated our own program. The children's club feet need to be slowly cast and recast every several weeks until they are recast into a somewhat near normal position. We have hired a Haitian nurse to manage and run the program. It has been one of our greatest successes in Haiti over the years we have been there.

Then, there are those patients that are carried into the clinic on someone's shoulders or backs or those that are carried on stretchers because whatever medical condition they have does not allow them to walk anymore. The best we can do sometimes is a wheelchair, crutches, a cane, or a walker. Think about trying to use any of these devices in the rough and tough Haitian environment, but we can surely leave it up to the Haitians to find a way to make it work. No matter what, one can hardly describe the look of surprise and satisfaction on their faces and in their eyes when we hand over a walking aid device to the patients.

Now that I have covered ways to get around in Haiti, I will spend some time on notable travel adventures I have experienced while in Haiti.

That Really Happened in Haiti!

Almost every year that I have travelled to Haiti, there have been dramatic turns of events and beyond belief experiences. Some team members have called these travels "harrowing." The following are my most memorable trips.

The Pay Loader

I mentioned this experience earlier, but it is worth fleshing out some more. Of those who went on that trip to Haiti in 1996, only Pat and

Bernie had been to Haiti before. Flying out to Jeremie was not much of a hassle at all, except for the goings on at the small airport, especially since a plane had just crashed there a few days before. The road trip from Jeremie to Leon was not quite what I expected with the road having been washed away and wiped out by the previous hurricane in many places. The normal 45 minute trip seemed to take hours, but we finally made it to the river that Leon sits on across the bridge. The immediate problem was that there was no bridge. I noticed the former bridge quite impressively piled up downstream. A foot bridge consisting of two long logs was being constructed for temporary access across the river. It would not be operational for a least a few more days. Several Haitians prepared to carry us across on their shoulders. At that moment, the pay loader appeared, and the driver lowered the bucket. We all climbed in, including Pastor Worch. Pastor Worch had recently had a heart attack but agreed to go to Haiti since I was a pharmacist and could take care of him if something happened. Well, at least I was certainly in the bucket with him and other members of the team. After the bucket was raised with all of us inside, someone took a picture. To me, this would become the most memorable of all pictures ever taken while I was in Haiti. It is the picture that appears on the back cover of the book.

We easily made it across the river and were deposited on the remainder of the road to Leon. All we had to do was carry our small travel bags the rest of the way. Our Haitian partners carried all of our heavy stuff plus several cases of made-from-real-sugar Coke in original 16 ounce glass bottles that Pastor Jean Antoine bought especially for us to make us feel at home. Indeed, we felt at home. When we left after several days, we walked down to the end of the road on the Leon side of the river not knowing what exactly to expect. The foot bridge was completed, and vehicles were waiting on the other side to take us back. We gingerly walked across our new bridge.

Next Year's Trip Back from Leon to Jeremie

The vehicular bridge was completed by the time we got to Leon the next year. I was now prepared for the road from Jeremie to Leon. It was actually worse the second year, but I was prepared mentally for it and did OK. What I was prepared for was the possibility of motion sickness, so I took my Benadryl for sure (I have since added ginger capsules and pressure wrist bands to my motion sickness regimen).

During my childhood, my father smoked cigars and cigarettes. He smoked all the time, including when he drove us around in the car. It was what everyone did back in those days. I started getting motion sickness from the cigarette smoke whenever I was in the car with my father. It was getting old for him when he had to stop on almost every trip, no matter how short, to let me jump out and throw up. To his credit, my father stopped smoking cigarettes altogether and concentrated on occasional cigars when I was not around. What this all seemed to do though was set me up for a lifetime of motion sickness. I learned little tricks to keep from getting nauseated like taking only short trips, sitting up in the car, taking deep breaths, sucking on mints, sipping ginger ale, eating hot French fries (they really do work for nausea), and opening my window to let in air, no matter how cold. Even breathing fumes from trucks and buses on the outside seemed to help. I get motion sickness in cars, on buses, on trains (even the Washington DC Metro subway—really bad when hot and jerky inside), on planes (ever ride on a Black Hawk Helicopter sideways and almost upside down at obscene speeds?), on amusement rides, especially on any kind of boat (including Coast Guard buoy tenders), and sadly even on playground swings. This did not bode well for travel in Haiti.

On the morning of our departure from Jeremie to go back to Leon, I ate the traditional Haiti breakfast of spaghetti with butter, but no sauce, and a cup of coffee. Basically plain spaghetti was to me a readily available alternative for hot French fries (source of potentially helpful complex carbohydrates, however that worked). The trip would be short even if on nasty roads. It was then that I made two mistakes: I agreed to ride in the bed of the pickup truck and to ride backwards. I would be engulfed with fresh air as a bonus, though. Off we started, crossed the bridge, and were onto the main road. I lasted about a mile through several swaybacks when I yelled: Rete! Rete! Stop! Stop! I have never eaten spaghetti for breakfast since that day. I will not offer any other description of what happened next. I had indeed suffered the first one of many motion sicknesses in Haiti.

The Haitian Translator Who Never Ever Had Motion Sickness

I will remain on the hot topic of motion sickness, just not mine this time. On a later trip across Haiti, we had several of our Haitian translators travelling with us. I believe that no Haitian will ever admit to having motion sickness. In any case, we were on one of those very common hot and sweaty old van trips from Port-au-Prince to Leon. I always used my privilege of age, being team leader, and especially motion sickness to sit up front with the driver. Many times there would be three of us. Usually the third person was the smallest person on the team, almost always one of the women, who would basically straddle the gear shift box squished in between the driver and me. We would do this for the trip that lasted up to 12 hours. This time, though, it was just the driver and me since there was enough room for the rest of the travelers in the back of the van.

One of the translators sitting in the back started to complain that he was getting car/van sick. No one paid much attention as after all, he was Haitian, and Haitian men do not get car sick. He kept saying he had to sit up front. Maybe he was just trying to jockey himself into a better seat. He was told that I really do get car sick, and I was not going to give him my seat. Knowing what the nausea of motion sickness can do to you (and I was at that point holding up very well),

I offered to switch seats with him. That we did. I climbed into the back of the van. Because of the stifling heat, all windows in the van were open, front, side and back. After several minutes on the road, those of us riding in the back of the van felt this spray come though the right side windows in the back of the van. It hit me in the face and dried immediately. I looked at one of the other team members, and his glasses were all dull yellow speckled. The translator had stuck his head out of the front passenger window and let out the contents of his stomach. The vomit glided along the outside of the van and was sucked into the back of the van. It dried so fast, we could literally scrape it off of us, but not before we came the closest to throwing someone out of a moving vehicle.

The Short Trip from Leon to Jeremie with Pere Jean Antoine

The telling of the story about this trip will be as short as the trip was in miles. On one of our trips from Leon to Jeremie, Pere Jean Antoine was able to drive his vehicle to give us a ride into Jeremie. I have mentioned how aggressive Haitian drivers could be. Pere Jean Antoine could be an assertive driver when need be, but he never was aggressive. He was courteous to all other drivers on the road and especially to pedestrians, who happen to be the target of almost every driver. We were coming down the winding road and got behind a vehicle being driven very slowly, even for Haiti standards. Pere Jean Antoine patiently followed behind until he got the opportunity to pass, which he did. The car he passed began to inch closer to us from behind until he was right behind our car. We felt a bump from behind and then a stronger bump that did some damage to Pere Jean Antoine's vehicle. Both vehicles came to a stop. I am not sure if the other driver recognized Pere Jean Antoine as a priest. In any case, priest or not, the other driver got a stern (to put it mildly) lecture about what just happened. There was damage to the car, and the other driver had to show his registration and insurance papers. I never forgot this incident because of the sheer strangeness of this whole event of bumper cars.

The First Long Trip Across Haiti

There were times when it was not practical to fly on the plane in Haiti and times the planes were not flying. The only viable alternative is to drive. No first time visitor is completely prepared for a 150 to 180 mile continuous road trip in Haiti. This trip makes my memorable trip list because it was the first. When we use trucks or vans to travel to our clinic site, we can not only take all of our team members, but we can also take all of our luggage and medical supplies and not have to worry about not getting everything on a small plane with us. The trucks we use are usually Toyota club cab type pickup trucks with short beds with four wheel drive and heavy duty Hangook Korean tires. The inside of the cab is very small, yet we will usually fit in six or seven people. Sometimes, if there is extra room in the bed, some of us will ride on top of the strapped-down cargo. I believe we usually max out with ten people in and on the truck, although we usually end up picking up several passengers on the road. Our convoy consists of two or usually three trucks on most occasions. The trip is long, hot, sweaty, cramped, damp, and sometimes smelly. We stop for gas, for rest stops (sometimes along side of the road), snacks, and rarely a full, or somewhat full, meal. The town of Les Cayes, 120 miles from Port-au-Prince, is the halfway stop between Port-au-Prince and Leon time wise, not distance wise. The time to Les Cayes is approximately four hours, yet it will be another four hours at least to make the last 60 miles to Jeremie. Most of the road is paved between Port-au-Prince to Les Cayes. The road from Les Cayes to Jeremie is another story. When we first went to Haiti, most of the road between Les Cayes and Jeremie was not paved, which made for slow, tortuous travel. As of today, approximately 60 percent is paved with the rest to be finished in the next decade.

Our meal, once we got to Les Cayes, was to be at a fancy (for Haiti) restaurant that served pizza. What could go wrong with that? I would not have recognized it as pizza if someone had not told me it was. It was kind of small, sparse, and yellowish in color. No matter though, as the ubiquitous Coke with the real sugar in the 16 ounce bottle was available for just one American dollar (and still is all over Haiti). After finishing our meal fairly quickly, we were on the road again. The roads were no longer paved very shortly after we left the main street of Les Cayes. Grey dust spewed up everywhere behind us and in front of us when vehicles passed the other way. I noticed the clean laundry hung on cactus-like plants along the road covered in fine grey dust. I recall one trip, when at the end, the guys who were riding behind us all the way to Leon got out and looked like grey ghosts in the night. By the way, that grey powder coats both the outside and the inside of you.

Since we were in pickup trucks, we could move faster than big trucks and buses that would appear in front of us. We continually jockeyed around these huge vehicles while playing chicken with vehicles coming our way on the other side, that is, when there was another side. The road was beginning to not even look like a road anymore. It became narrower, overlooked sheer cliffs, rutted, boulder-strewn, water-logged, muddy, slippery, and everything in between. Then we came to our first real obstacle. The stream across the road was flowing rapidly with several feet of water (there is now a bridge there built as part of the new road construction). We had only three choices: try to drive through, wait a very long time, or go back. The drivers chose to drive through. I lived in Arizona for several years where dry washes filled up with several feet of rapidly rushing water in a very short time. Drivers not realizing the sheer force of such waters had been washed away. At this moment, this seemed like a real possibility for us. Yes, like those drivers in Arizona, the drivers did not like the alternative and were willing to take the chance. I am sure the Haitian drivers knew what their exact odds were for making it across, especially with a fully loaded truck. Drive through they did, and we made it. It was only after we got across that we were told the only reason we would not have made it would have been if a heavy boulder was being washed across the road at the exact same time we were crossing.

Rain while travelling is good in that it really cuts down on the dust and keeps the temperature down. It also cools down hot wheel bearings, as you will hear about in the last travel adventure. It is bad in that it causes rivers to rise, makes roads with grey dust very slippery, and fogs up windshields with poor defrosting systems or not having a towel to wipe the inside of the window. Through all these adventures, we never hit anything except a chicken in the town of Beaumont. It is my understanding there is no worse crime any driver can commit than killing a chicken crossing the road in Haiti. We wasted no time getting out of Beaumont.

After one of the most uneventful trips I have endured in Haiti, we arrived in Leon and crossed the new bridge. We drove onto the rectory grounds, stopped, and breathed a big sigh of relief. This was to be the first of dozens of these cross-country Haiti trips for me, which continue to today. The only thing is that I was 20 years younger back then.

The First Trip to Carcasse

On the first trip to Carcasse, we flew the small plane to Jeremie where we met the trucks to take us to Carcasse. It was late in the afternoon when we arrived, and we had to stop in Jeremie before driving on to Carcasse. It was about 6 PM and already getting dark when we headed out. It was my assumption and I think everyone else's, that Carcasse was not much farther from Jeremie than Leon. On that assumption, I did not reinforce my initial Benadryl dose for added motion sickness prevention. I also had a limited supply of mints. Then as darkness fell, time dragged on: one hour, two hours, and three hours. Just where were we? We could not see much as it was a dark night in Haiti. Finally, after going up and down a very high mountain range, we saw the ocean. We stopped a few moments to admire the scene.

One of our nurse practitioners and I were developing severe motion sickness, made worse by the travel in the dark with no frame of reference to anything. The unexpected stop had literally "saved our lives" at the moment. Then, we hit the road again. The two of us were once again sick out our minds, trying to hold it all in. All of the sudden, one of our tires went flat. We had to stop to replace the tire, which took a little while in the dark. The nurse practitioner and I were saved by the bell, I mean, the flat tire. We hit the road again, inching closer to Carcasse, when once again we had another flat tire. We were so happy because this was now going to take a long while as we had no spare tire left. As we propped ourselves against the hill along the road, we drew in the fresh air and collapsed. The other truck had to go onto Carcasse to get a new spare tire. After approximately an hour, it was back. The tire was replaced, and once again we hit the road for the last time. We arrived in downtown Carcasse (the rectory was right in the middle of the town) just after midnight. We had been on the road since 5 AM that morning in Washington, DC. Both the nurse practitioner and I made sure we took enough Benadryl on the trip back to Jeremie when the week was over.

The Bus To and From Carcasse

One year we decided to charter one of those big beautiful Haitian multi-colored buses as the best option to go to and from Carcasse. We could take as much medical supplies as we wanted on the bus, and the inside of the bus was more bearable than most road vehicles we endured in the past. Since we could get a good rate by doing a round trip, we decided to come back by bus rather than by plane, even though hauling medical supplies was not an issue.

The trip to Carcasse from Port-au-Prince on the bus was long as usual but somewhat more comfortable and refreshing than all previous trips. There was certainly enough room to stretch out even if the seats were not leather covered, plush, or permanently attached to the floor. I cannot say for sure as I was allowed to ride up front with the bus driver because I was number one on the motion sickness priority list. There was, as there always is in Haiti, good and bad about that privilege. I did not get sick for sure. From what I understand, being inside the bus was somewhat tomb-like. Being up front, I got to see and hear everything: the near misses with oncoming vehicles; how close a vehicle could get to a pedestrian and not hit him or her (once again this seemed to be part of the driving process in Haiti, no matter what size vehicle you were driving); how fast a bus this size could really go on narrow parts of the road in comparison to the bus' width; the missing by inches of going over the mountain side as we went around a curve on the narrower part of the road just outside of Carcasse; being able to listen to the hanging, unattached shock absorber banging on the passenger side of the bus, and having first opportunity to breathe in all road hazards. It was quite impressive, though, to pull into the town of Carcasse on this great big bus. On top of that, we would do it again to go back to Port-au-Prince. Of course, I thought, the hanging shock absorber would be fixed by then.

As always, the long hard days of work in Carcasse went quickly. The bus would be there very early Saturday morning to take us back. It showed up on time. As I opened the passenger door to climb up into the bus, I saw the cook sitting there. I handed her the "motion sickness get out of jail card," and she grudgingly got out and went into the main part of the bus. As I recall, several of the team members refused to ride the bus out of town until the windy mountain road cleared the first mountain range. Instead, they rode in a pickup truck to the top. I pondered as to how they also knew about narrowly-by-inches going over the side on the way in. I did not tell anyone about it until after the trip. I also checked out the hanging shock absorber; it was still swaying unattached in the wind.

It was definitely tougher going back. We were much more beat on the way back than the way to Carcasse. At least on the way to Carcasse, we were headed for the country. On the way back, we were headed to the city, quite a difference. We would arrive during rush hour in Port-au-Prince. Yes; there are more than enough vehicles to have a rush hour in Haiti, even on a Saturday afternoon/evening. The highlight for me sitting up front on the way back occurred as we went very fast around a blind curve on the paved portion of the road. It is a fact in Haiti that if you blow your horn loudly and often going around a blind curve, no approaching vehicle will be ever coming at you the other way. It had always worked up to this moment. As we entered the curve, what should be coming directly at us? Of course, it was a huge tractor trailer truck. It was time for immediate action. We went as far to the right as possible without going off the road using every inch of pseudo-shoulder available. The truck swings as far as possible to his right. Like ships passing in the night, the front of the bus misses the back of the tractor trailer by less inches than we missed going over the cliff in Carcasse. No one in the bus saw this other than the driver, his helper hanging on the side of the bus (he actually hung there the whole trip sometimes, moving to the top of the bus like Tom Cruise in Mission Impossible), and me.

There was another situation where a vehicle has passed our bus, and our driver was not happy about it, especially when one of the riders on the vehicle gave our bus driver the "what's up with you" sign. The vehicle that passed us was a tap-tap of some sort, and of course, people were hanging off the back. When the tap-tap now in front of us had to stop, the bus driver pulled up from behind to within inches of crushing the man. Around this time, a constant buzzer continued to well, buzz. Warning buzzers do not buzz unless they malfunction or really want to warn you about something serious. Most drivers hope it is a malfunction as you really want to get where you are going. We stopped, and the helper checked something. The buzzer stopped but then began buzzing a short time later. The driver stopped again and checked the brakes. From what I could understand, something was wrong with the brakes. We drove all the way back with the buzzer buzzing.

As anticipated, we hit Port-au-Prince at rush hour and crept our last miles agonizingly home to our guesthouse. Sadly, we moved so slowly we got a bird eye's view of the worst slums in all of Haiti. We passed food market stalls fed by plastic clogged drainage ditches and surrounded by rotting garbage and human waste. When we finally emerged from the bus, unloaded, and settled in, we noticed that whenever we coughed, we coughed up grey sputum, and whenever we blew our noses, grey mucous came out, that day and the next. After that bus trip, we decided we would never do a round trip on the bus again. One way out to Carcasse with all of our supplies would be acceptable, but we would fly back next time. I have to admit, the bus driver did know how to navigate that bus over and through the nastiest of roads, trails, and paths.

Finally, A First Class Bus Trip

Because the airline in Haiti is currently bankrupt and out of business, you obviously cannot fly between Port-au-Prince and Jeremie. Those on the ground have taken quick notice and quick advantage of the situation. There are now modern air-conditioned buses (well, actually, big van type buses) plying the roads that were previously flown over by the planes. That is not exactly true as the planes fly a straight line between the two cities while road vehicles must follow the only road that goes south from Port-au-Prince before it goes back north from Les Cayes to Jeremie.

On my last trip to Haiti, I made it to the bus depot in Jeremie thanks to Benson and his dirt bike. Benson dropped me off at the depot. Honore was there to meet me and bid me farewell. My engineering student friend, Pierre Louis, was also there to accompany me on the bus to make sure I would get to where I was to go. The day started pleasantly as we munched on free pates and coffee in the depot before the bus departed. The bus was not too full at that time as we would be picking up some additional passengers on the way. I was able to select a seat near the back next to the window with Pierre Louis sitting in the aisle seat beside me. I felt pretty good about the seat as I would now be able to lean my head against the inside of the bus and maybe even nod off for a while. That was a very bad decision. When I got into the seat, I found the hump of the back wheel well right under me. That forced my knees up to near my chin. I was essentially molded into the bus structure and would be for the next four hours. My legs and feet began to cramp as I tried to move any part of my body at all if possible to avoid the pain. I also had to pee eventually, but the bus was not stopping. In addition, the air conditioning was not strong enough to hit me away from the aisle. Even though pumped up with Benadryl, ginger, pressure wrist bands, and free pate and coffee, I became hot, sweaty, and nauseated, holding my contents in, as this bus was not going to stop to let me out until it was good and ready. Pierre Louis was my host in a way, and I did not want to disturb him, so I endured.

Finally, as we entered a busy street of a bustling town, Pierre Louis informed me that we would stop briefly to relieve ourselves. I got out with about half the people on the bus to pee. Where was the toilet? There was none. We were on the very busy main street, and men from the bus were peeing in hedges along the road. I walked a short distance away to try and find some privacy. I did as I walked into someone's front yard and saw three of the female passengers squatting and peeing. I slowly backed out but did notice it was the most private place around. After the three women came out, I rushed into the hidden yard. The feeling was great when I was done. I rushed back to the bus and got on. Would you not know it, but about two miles down the road, the bus stopped at a restaurant with separate men and women indoor bathrooms?

I figured it could have been worse like the time we were on a mountain road on another trip and stopped to let everyone pee. In the mountains, it is much easier to find a private spot. I walked a short distance from the vehicle, found my private spot, and immediately had my left feet drop down into a hole up to my groin. All I could think was that I would be swallowed up by the earth and never be found again. My right foot held the high ground, and I was able to pull my other foot out with some effort. I never knew what that hole was for because I was too embarrassed to tell anyone what had just happened. Maybe now, someone will tell me.

After the restaurant and bathroom stop, I got back on the bus with Pierre Louis and told him that my six foot, two-inch frame would not survive the rest of the trip unless I sat in his aisle seat. Pierre Louis graciously swapped seats with me, and I am still here to travel once again in Haiti.

The Most Notorious Trip of All

When I got back from this trip to Haiti, it was so memorable and so notorious, I wrote the following newsletter article about it (somewhat modified for this book).

This is a synopsis of our trip to Haiti:
1. The plane engine caught on fire after we landed on a cliffside dirt runway in Jeremie, Haiti.
2. The plane was still on the ground waiting for a new engine from the US when we were scheduled to leave a week later. After getting back to the United States, we learned that the engine was never replaced and that the airline had filed for bankruptcy. We had flown on the last plane ever up to now to Jeremie.
3. We had to drive all the way back at the end of the mission (11 hours) after getting up at 2 AM and had a very bad trip from Jeremie to Les Cayes.
4. The police and/or gunmen stopped us twice at roadblocks. They were not dressed in police uniforms. Some wore khakis, and some wore headbands. They had what appeared to be AK-47s. I was, as usual, seated up front with the driver. Motion sickness gets you a front seat view of all the action. One of the gunmen stuck his head in a back window to check out the occupants. An anonymous team member

told the gunman that this was not acceptable in the United States. The gunman told the anonymous passenger that this was not the United States. Other passengers in the car told the anonymous team member to keep her mouth shut. While this was going on in the back, it was even more intense up front. Another gunman asked the driver for the vehicle registration information. The driver fumbled around and finally found it. The gunman was not satisfied with the papers. He asked for the insurance information. It was an unusually cool night in Haiti, but the driver was sweating profusely. He could not find the papers as he was the Bishop's driver, but he was driving our Pastor's car. He finally found those papers but was still having problems identifying who he was and why he was driving the car. The gunmen only let us go when the Bishop's driver threatened to call the Bishop and wake him up at 2:30 in the morning. Evidently, the gunmen did not want to risk waking up the Bishop of Jeremie. We were stopped at another road block, but this time we passed through with a real police car following us for several miles as an apparent escort.

5. After the first roadblock, the back wheel got very hot as the wheel bearings were bad. The driver made several valiant attempts to jar the wheel bearings so they would not melt and fuse. Fortunately, the paved portion of the road ran out, and we were now driving on the original non-paved rutted dirt road. It has just rained ahead of us, so the roads were wet and muddy. The vehicle did not flip over the side of the mountain as the rough road jostled the bearings while the puddles from the downpour cooled them off.

6. At the very end of the trip, the brakes also locked up, and the vehicle would not go at one point as smoke poured out of the two front wheels.

7. We just barely rolled into the near vicinity of the bus station, but the same anonymous team leader got us on the wrong

bus. Fortunately it went to Port-au-Prince although to the wrong terminal.

8. We finally figured out we were on the wrong bus because we were at the wrong terminal because there was no one there to pick us up to take us to the airport. Our very confused bus driver even offered to take us to the airport, but we finally made contact with the correct bus company.

9. We did see over 1,000 patients during our week in Haiti and helped a lot of sick people as always.

Chapter 6

The Animals of Haiti

Animals Large and Small

Believe it or not, animals play a large role in our Haiti medical missions. The animals I will talk about are not unusual to most countries, including the United States. Some are common household pets. Some are uncommon household pets. Some are just good old common household pests. Most team members when they come to Haiti will develop a relationship with these pets and pests, whether they wish to or not.

Dogs I Have Known

Dogs appear to play unique roles in Haitian society, but I am not quite sure what they are. They certainly have played unique roles in the lives of our medical missionaries and mine. It seems like every rectory or house with a priest in it has a dog or several dogs. I assume they are there to protect and guard the property and make a lot of noise when someone is around as a general alert. Dogs are the only "pets" that I see in any number out on the streets, especially in the countryside. Almost every dog you see looks like a scarecrow. Since you hardly ever see any overweight Haitians, I do not know why their dogs should be fat like many dogs in America. Dogs in Haiti come and go quickly also. I do not recall meeting and knowing any dog in Haiti for more than two trips running.

Recalling my remembrances of Dentist Jack, you will recall the first Haitian dog I ever met intimately. Like most dogs I have known in Haiti, he would disappear during the day doing whatever dogs do during the day (sleeping?), but would always reappear at dusk around dinner time. Dogs in Haiti seem to have good table manners and do not badger people while eating. They do start barking it up after dark and especially in the deep of the night. The nameless dog

I first met fit the Haitian dog mold perfectly. I never knew the name of any dog in Haiti, even if they do have names. You just described them by their size and color if there were more than one dog. Otherwise, you just called them "the dog." This first dog that I met did not distinguish himself in any particular way until Dentist Jack fell over him.

Over the years, dogs came and went with regularity. There were only a few years that no living dog was around during our mission visits. Many years passed before I became intimate with any other rectory dogs. Pere Verdieu had two dogs on his property. One was a huge black Rottweiler while the other was a small, innocent enough looking white-colored dog. Both dogs stayed pretty much out of sight, with the Rottweiler staying more secluded. With his impressive size, I was fine with that. Somewhat out of the mold, the small dog would hang around a fair amount during the day. Again, at dusk, both dogs would make an appearance. At night, as soon as our heads would hit the pillows, one of the dogs would start barking periodically for what seemed like the whole night. After several nights of this, we could stand it no longer. We talked with Pere Verdieu, but it seemed like there was not a whole lot he could do. So when the Rottweiler appeared that evening, we were sure it had to be the barking dog. It took us forever to load some food with a 50 mg dose of Benadryl to put him to sleep for a night. It took so long to drug him, not because he was so fearsome, but he was just so smart knowing we had put something in his food. Finally, he took the bite, and those of us who drugged the dog high-fived each other. We hit the pillows and shortly after falling asleep, we heard the dog barking again. That time I went out to see if I could find the dog, and indeed I did. We drugged the wrong dog. The next evening Pere Verdieu roped and dragged the small dog up to the school about one-half mile away. We slept in peace finally. A dog that was so smart to fool us into drugging the wrong dog would not be away for long. He was back the next night. The next year we came back the Rottweiler was dead, but the small dog was to be around for one more time. He was dragged up to the school every night we were there to always return well before morning.

There is another Carcasse dog story, or I should say, dogs' story. One night we were all asleep for about an hour, when around midnight, we heard a sound beyond belief. It was the approaching sound of some type of howling whirlwind that was roaring through town. It had to be every dog in town in a huge posse passing though the street. The sound was like the Hound of Baskervilles in Sherlock Holmes multiplied many times over. Then, it was all over, never to be repeated to this day. We never figured it out, although I bet the ghost of the small dog was at the head of the pack.

Finally, there was Dead Dog. I saw Dead Dog alive for only a few moments of his life. We were driving up to a drugstore to get some supplies. Dead Dog ran across the Jeremie Street just in time to be run over by the vehicle in front of us. Road kill in Haiti basically stay where they went down, and the drivers speed on. This was the case with Dead Dog. We parked in front of the drugstore for a while. Dead Dog remained on the pavement, well, dead. Eventually, an older lady saw Dead Dog. She found a cardboard box and a type of shovel. She tried repeatedly to scoop up Dead Dog into the cardboard box. Eventually, she succeeded. I was transfixed by the lady's mournful eyes and the saga of only this woman being willing to drag the dog off the road. Such is life in Haiti.

Cats I Have Fed Under the Table

Being a cat person, I have always fed a lot of cats under the table. Cats are good for picking up scraps, and Haitian cats are no different. Unlike dogs, which you saw roaming the streets, I never saw a cat doing so in Haiti. The only cats I ever saw were rectory cats. I believe it was a given that the cats were there to keep the mice away. Every cat I saw in Haiti was young (if not a kitten), scrawny, and eternally hungry. I never saw the same cat two years in a row. I assumed most died of starvation or got eaten by some wild animal. There had to be adult cats making new kittens, but I never saw them. Food is definitely scarce in Haiti, and one does not want to "waste" food on cats. Even so, I could not resist scraping the final scraps of meat off the chicken bone to slip to the cat under the table. I would just have eaten the final scrap myself anyway. All cats, even scrawny cats, like everyone, especially those people who do not like cats. It was worth feeding the kittens to keep them alive for when we were there to keep the mice away from my food and to aggravate people, such as the anonymous team member who just did not like cats.

Mice That Got Away

It must have been the time there were no cats around in Carcasse, now that I think about it. I would take wheat crackers in those packets of six crackers with cheese or peanut butter. They made great snacks when there was no time to eat a scheduled meal or to give to children and other hungry people I met on the road. Even with the plastic wrapping, I knew bugs could get into the crackers, so I put my stash on a high concrete ledge above the wall in my bedroom. The next day I went to get a pack to eat, the plastic was torn and several crackers were eaten. All I could think was that some kid got into the room, found the crackers, and ate some. That had actually happened on one mission trip. So I counted up losses and finished off the remaining crackers in the pack. The next day, the same thing happened. I wondered how I was ever going to catch the culprit. The next day when I woke up, my roommate said to me that he had seen mice running up and down my wall for several nights while I was sleeping. I thanked him for taking so long to let me know and could only think about the remaining crackers I ate after the mice were there first.

Roosters in the Night and Chickens at Day

Growing up as a child in my small hometown, almost everyone had a chicken coop and at least one rooster. Roosters in Northeastern

Pennsylvania tended to only crow at dawn and occasionally during the day. I do not recall hearing any roosters at night. Haiti is definitely not Northeastern Pennsylvania. Haiti has a lot of roosters. Haiti has a lot of loud roosters who know how to strut. They begin really crowing around 2 or 3 in the morning. One brave rooster starts the cacophony, and the crescendo rolls across the valley from one mountain to the next mountain and begins the journey back to the original rooster. The length and time and number of cycles of the journey depend upon the number of active roosters involved. This can go on for a long time, especially when you are trying to sleep.

Chickens also can on occasion form a more intimate relationship with you. I have woken up several times in Haiti with a chicken sleeping next or near to me. They did not seem to mind me at all. One day, walking back from a visit with one of my friends, a mother chicken was walking off the side of the road with her brood of chicks. I wondered just how many peeps are in a normal brood of Haitian chickens, so I counted them. After counting, I proudly told my friend how many peeps were in the brood. He nearly fell over when I told him. I wondered what caused his startled reaction. He whispered to me that to count the number of peeps in a brood would result in the near future death of the peeps. I had just condemned his neighbor's chickens!

Monster Spiders

Monster spiders are common in Haiti, and they seem to like being near people. Two of these spiders have had close-by relationships with me. The first monster spider I ever met in Haiti was in the outside bathroom at the Carcasse rectory. It would hang out behind the small mirror on the wall and come out mainly at night. I did not know what he did when he went back behind the mirror. I was not about to take the mirror off the wall to find out. That spider was there for several years running, or it was a close relative the later years. We looked at each other, but that is as far as we ever went.

Truthfully, I despise spiders, even knowing they eat a lot of bad insects, and I will squash any spider I can with any available weapon. Not that spider; I had a whole lot of respect for him.

The second monster spider I met lived in or on the wall of my room at Fosy's school in Leon. Fosy gave me a choice of rooms to sleep in, and of course, I chose the one with the spider. I was about to turn off the battery operated light when I saw him on the wall at the front of my room just over the door. No room in Haiti is ever sealed completely, so I knew the spider came in from somewhere and could go back out. I knew from past experience that if I did not bother these guys, they will not bother me. When I woke up in the morning, monster spider was gone, and for good, I hoped. The next night he was there again. I just had to do better. I went over to him and encouraged him to go over the wall and into someone else's room. He did, and I did not see him again. I only heard about him from another team member in a nearby room.

Note: When I went back in 2016, the spider or one of his descendants was back. On two different nights, I saw him crawling on the wall. Twice I tried to get him out of the room, and twice he hid under my bed. I figured: live and let live for the both of us.

There's a Frog (Could It Be a Prince?) in My Bed

One evening we heard a loud scream from the room of one of our anonymous team members. I thought for sure she had seen a monster spider. As she emerged from her room, she shouted out that there was a frog in her bed. I walked into the room and saw this princely-looking frog forlornly looking up at me. I left him in peace for the moment and went back out. Of course, I told the anonymous team member that she should go back in and kiss the frog, and she would become a Haitian princess. She did not and still remains prince-less, but ah; there would be yet a second chance.

Many years later, on our most recent trip to Haiti, this same team member calmly came out of her room and told me there was something in there. I could have guessed a lot of creatures, but I had remembered that previously rejected prince frog. I asked her if it was a frog, and she said yes. Having already now been rejected a second time, the frog had moved to the window sill. For one last time, he peered into my eyes sadly just before I showed him out the window. These two times have been the only times I have seen a frog in Haiti.

No Snakes?

There are no snakes in Haiti (Note: this is controversial). I have never seen one.

Let's Not Forget the Insects

Insects are animals and play a large role in intimate contacts with missionaries in Haiti.

Mosquitoes

Mosquitoes are everywhere in Haiti but seem to be the worst in the cities. I get bitten more in Port-au-Prince and Jeremie than I ever do in Leon and Carcasse. There are two kinds of missionaries that come to Haiti: those that use mosquito nets or contraptions and those that do not use mosquito nets or contraptions. By contraptions, I mean those expandable and foldable things that pop open but do not as easily pop back. Think of windshield heat deflectors that you try to put on your car windshield on hot sunny days and think even more about trying to fold them back to their original size and shape. I personally do not use nets and would not use them even if the contraptions easily went back to their original forms. As far as I am concerned, all they do is allow a few mosquitoes inside to spend the night with you. More women than men tend to use them, and I think I know why. The unique hormones that women possess really attract mosquitoes. Another reason for me not to use the nets is that most of the mosquitoes are already with the women and are ignoring me. More than not, female medical team members outnumber male members by two to one.

Mosquitoes do carry malaria, dengue fever, and chikungunya. All of them are nasty parasites, with malaria being the worst. For malaria prophylaxis, we take chloroquine tablets for two weeks before we go to Haiti, for the weeks we are in Haiti, and for four weeks after we get back from Haiti. They are taken for only one day of the week on the same day each week. To date, only one team member has come back with dengue fever. Not one of us came down with chikungunya when it was an epidemic in Haiti. Chikungunya is an illness caused by a virus that spreads through mosquito bites. The most common symptoms of chikungunya are fever and joint pain. Dengue fever (Breakbone fever) is a disease transmitted by a mosquito bite. Dengue fever is a severe, flu-like illness that affects infants, young children, and adults, but seldom causes death.

As an additional precaution, despite the heat, I wear socks and long sleeve shirts and pants to bed at night. Even though I sweat more, this maneuver helps save me from another ubiquitous insect, the bedbug.

Bedbugs

Bedbugs are slyer than mosquitoes. You can hear and see and really feel the bite of mosquitoes. Bedbugs literally sneak up on you. You may feel the bites at night, but it could also just be beads of sweat rolling down your body. You might feel itchy, but it might just be the rough sheets. You may not even know you had contact until you get back home and notice all the tiny red spots all over your body. Everyone tells you about the mosquitoes; hardly anyone tells you about the bedbugs. Mosquito nets keep out a lot of mosquitoes, but they keep out no bedbugs. The best and only thing that I have found that keeps bedbugs out of bed with me is a cinnamon-based spray.

Yes, your bed sheets will smell like a pumpkin spice latté, but it is a small price to pay.

Roaches

I hate roaches, a.k.a. cockroaches, as much as I hate all insects and arachnoids. They look just plain ugly. The roaches of Haiti are not as fast as the roaches of New Orleans or as big as the roaches of Philadelphia. They usually do not crawl in bed with you like the roaches of New Orleans or are as invasive or adaptive as the roaches of Philadelphia. Nonetheless, they are nasty-looking and crunch just as loud as the roaches of New Orleans and Philadelphia. When I lived in New Orleans and in Philadelphia, there were just too many to kill personally. You depended upon the exterminator to do his monthly job. Since I do not like to personally crunch roaches, I usually also live and let them live in Haiti. So, roaches were not an issue until a recent trip.

Several strong, male students were sharing a room for the first night of the mission. I heard one of them say that their room was unacceptable because they had seen several roaches. I told them to kill them to make their room acceptable. They said they could not do that. I asked them why? They could face nasty-looking spiders and all other insects, but they could not face roaches. That is when I learned about katsaridaphobia, the serious fear of roaches. Actually, I could not understand how two grown men could be afraid of roaches. While we were having our discussion on katsaridaphobia, one of the female team members came in and crunched the two roaches after running them down (the roaches, that is).

Ants

Ants, and similar small insects, appear out of nowhere in Haiti just like they do anywhere. Only, in Haiti they appear all year round while in the Northeastern United States, we just have to deal with them in the warm and hot months. Ants and similar small insects of unknown names appear in Haiti, just like anywhere else, where there is food. The trick seems to be to keep your food in sealed containers. The ants of Haiti hardly ever have to deal with sealed containers as it is nearly impossible to seal anything. You can keep fruit flies off food stuffs by putting those special colored Haitian plastic domes over your food as it sits out on the table. During my first trip to Haiti, I found out that unless you have something hermetically sealed, the bugs will eventually get in. I had taken a "can" of cashews with me to snack on. A can of cashews is actually a cardboard container with a metal bottom and a plastic top. For several days, I ate rationed portions of the cashews to make them last over the whole trip. On the third day, as I was eating my next portion, I kind of swished around the nuts at the bottom. To my surprise, it was crawling with these tiny, six-legged creatures. Totally grossed out, I wondered how many of them (the creatures) I had eaten. Sadly, I dumped out the remaining cashews and tiny creatures.

Haitian Animals I Saw But Did Not Touch

I did not develop a relationship with every animal that I saw. Actually, United States Customs asks you if you had any contact with farm animals while in Haiti, and I did not want to say yes and not get back into the United States! Here is my animal list:

All birds of the air and in the trees; conch; fish and crustaceans (well, I did eat a few) in the river or the sea; insects (I did eat a few; there was also the cricket that crawled over my face one night in bed); spiders; frogs; lizards, chickens; roosters; goats; cows; bulls, ducks; burros/donkeys; mules (sorry, I do not really know the differences except for mules even though I talked about them, I did not know any personally); sheep (at least I saw some); horses (few); pigs (quite a few); dogs; cats (I may have touched a few giving them scraps); and mice.

Haitian Animals That I Ate

Last, and not least, is a list of those unfortunate animals that I have eaten in Haiti: chickens and their eggs, goats, cows, pigs (including bladder and intestines), lobster (not conch, which I never ate), shrimp, fish, and ants.

My most eaten animal is the chicken; I have probably eaten more ants than all the rest of the animals combined.

Chapter 7

At Last: The Best and The Worst of My Stories

The Worst of The Worst

I have already told several tales and stories that did not reflect the best of times in Haiti for me. There are several mores stories that I want to tell that had dramatic effects on me and my understanding of how tough and difficult life is in Haiti. So, here goes:

The Goat Bladder and Intestines in Leon

The first meal that I was served on the first night we were in Leon included the delicacy of goat intestines cooked in the goat's bladder. At least that is what I was told it was, and I truly believe it was exactly that. I was excited as I sat down to my first home-cooked meal in Haiti. I recognized the beans and rice and the chicken and vegetables. I did not recommend the "main" course. It was some kind of round, tied off bag-looking object sitting in the middle of the plate. When it was cut open, some kind of warm, worm-like looking objects slid out onto the plate. They had a somewhat putrid smell that reminded me of the first time I ever smelled and tried venison or the smell you get from bad lamb. It seemed like the small objects were still moving. So, I asked my favorite anonymous team member, what was it? She replied that it was a Haitian delicacy and to just try it. I did and was able to get a few pieces down. I do not recall anyone eating any, which I thought was strange. I finished my meal and within hours, I was nauseated and cramped up. Then the vomiting and diarrhea started. It seemed to be endless and forever. I could not believe I came all the way to Haiti to die within a few days. Toilets in Haiti clog easily and are far and few in between. Pere Jean Antoine let me use his personal toilet, which I used over and over into the night. Periodically, to her credit, the anonymous team member would come into the bathroom and clean everything up.

I recovered enough to at least make it to the supper table the next evening. The leftover bladder from the past night's meal reappeared. No one ate any as on the third evening when again it appeared. It was never to be seen again. Well, the original serving was gone, but the next year when we sat down for our first meal in Leon, the main attraction was goat intestines in goat bladder. We respectfully requested that Pere Jean Antoine remove it from all future menus, which he graciously did.

The Conch in Carcasse

Carcasse is on the northeastern seashore of Haiti. Lobster is common, but not as common as conch for eating. Conch is served at least once per trip in Carcasse for supper. On the day it was being served, some boys had caught a lobster and gave it to one of their favorite doctors on the medical team. She brought the lobster to the cook at the rectory to prepare for her. Knowing I had enjoyed lobster while stationed in Maine, the doctor brought a chunk of it for me to eat. From my vast Maine experience of having eaten hundreds of lobsters, I knew it had been cooked perfectly (as a matter of fact, it was one of the most perfectly cooked lobsters I had ever seen and eaten). On the same day, the cook had gone to the next town over to buy some conch at the market place for supper. I wondered how long the conch had been exposed to the heat on the way back from the market place. Then, after it had been prepared and put out on the table, I wondered how long it had been cooked. It had that "goat's intestine in bladder" smell. I told the others who were there about my previous experience, suggesting they avoid the conch. Some did listen, but most did not. By late evening, those who did not listen were lining up for the only available toilet, which was right outside my bedroom door. The line continued all night. By the next day, a handful of team members were out of commission. My advice to anyone in Haiti remains that if the food smells bad and looks like it is still moving do not eat it.

A Short, Very Sad Airplane Story

I already told of the first time that we landed in Haiti of the small plane that had crashed at the end of the runway. When you are in Haiti, not much news gets in, and not much news gets out. When I left Haiti, I did not know the final outcome of the plane crash. When I was going through Customs, the agent asked me from where I was coming from. I told him Haiti. He asked me if I knew anything about a plane crash in Haiti. I told him what I knew. He then told me what he knew. Several days before, the wife of the pilot came home with the remains of her husband.

A Longer, Better Outcome Airplane Story

Approximately ten years ago, we landed at the airport in Miami late as usual. In fact, until that time, we had never made the next scheduled flight back to Washington, DC. This time, we had a chance, small as it was. The other pharmacist who had gone to Haiti with me was a coworker of mine at the National Institutes of Health. He was young and fast, and I was old and fast. To our added advantage, we had no checked in luggage to wait to arrive and get it through Customs. We started running to Immigration and Customs. As we made it through both, my pharmacist friend realized he left his cell phone in Customs. He told me to run ahead and see if I could hold the plane for him, that is, if I made it in time. I raced ahead and got to the gate. It was still open. I explained to the counter agent what was happening. Beyond belief, she agreed to hold the gate open for a few more minutes. While we were waiting, she told me that the airline already knows that no one from a Haiti flight ever makes a connecting flight to Washington, DC and that it automatically holds seats open on the next scheduled flight (wonder if that is still done ten years later). In the meantime, my friend comes huffing and puffing, and we get on the plane. Did we ever feel smug and victorious. We broke the long-standing record and made the next flight. Just wait until we got home and would get to gloat with all those who did not make the flight and were left behind.

The flight home was very peaceful. I saw some of the most gorgeous views I had ever seen on an airplane as I looked out my window to the west watching the sun set below the horizon and clouds. The flashes and hues of the light off the clouds at the horizon were indescribable and beyond belief. I let it all slowly and majestically sink in. It was time to make our landing at Reagan National Airport. As we began our approach and began to descend on the runway, we suddenly became airborne again. I knew the runways at Reagan are shorter than most airports, and I had experienced this once before when there was a runway issue. Evidently, this time it was not a runway issue but a plane issue. The pilot announced that we were not landing at Reagan but were being diverted to Dulles International Airport for an emergency landing.

We were not told what the emergency was. I assumed it had something to do with the landing mechanism and/or the wheels. Off we headed to Dulles, a very short distance away in miles. Then we started circling for approximately an hour. I assume we were burning off excess fuel. Finally, it was announced that we were going to land. As the plane got closer to Dulles, I could not see any runways until I finally saw this runway out in the boondocks. Next to the runway, I could see fire trucks and emergency vehicles with flashing lights. We touched ground on the runway and came to a stop. We sat there for a while. I looked out and saw that the runway was adjacent to the maintenance facilities. I could not see the control tower anywhere in sight. We then got out by walking down the long roll up ladders like the ones still being used at the Haiti airport. One of those huge Mitsubishi Heavy Industries Crystal Mover Vehicles a.k.a. Mobile Lounges pulled up. We had landed safely but at the wrong destination airport. My friend called his wife, who was now at Reagan waiting to pick us up. I arrived home well after midnight.

The next day I found out that the rest of our fellow travelers made the next scheduled flight after the one we made and arrived home well before midnight. The next day, I got an email from the airline stating that it was sorry for the inconvenience that was caused and it would do better next time. There was not a word about what had happened and why. I did hear later from a friend of mine that there was a 15-second story on the news about an emergency landing at Dulles.

A Machete at the Airport

On one trip to Haiti, I was sponsoring a girl in the Dominican Republic, so I decided to extend my stay on Hispaniola and go to see the girl in Santo Domingo. The visit went very well. The last day, I headed out to the airport with my carry on and my check in bag. I barely made it to the airport in time and rushed through the metal detector. I was stopped by the pre-9/11 guard. He showed me the x-ray of my carry on and asked if I knew what the metal object laying on the bottom of my bag was. When I saw the outline, I knew immediately it was the Haitian machete that I bought and put into my bag and entirely forgot about. This is how the story played back then. No, I was not immediately arrested and thrown into a Dominican jail cell. The guard pulled out a box that my machete fit into perfectly. He then sealed the box and gave me a receipt. He told me he would give it to the pilot of the plane, and the pilot would give it back to me as I deplaned in the United States. As I was getting off, I gave the pilot my receipt and was handed the perfectly boxed machete.

Dirty Rotten Haitian Money

The Gourde (HTG), a.k.a. Goude, is the official currency of Haiti. The gourde can be further subdivided into 100 cents. The gourde was formerly pegged to the US dollar at a rate of five (5) gourdes to one US dollar. Since then, however, the gourde has been placed on a floating rate. In light of the former peg, five gourdes are often referred to as a "Haitian dollar." Five cents, in similar nature, is referred to as a "Haitian penny." In select regions of Haiti, prices are denoted in Haitian dollars rather than gourdes. Customers are left to multiply the dollars by five. Banknotes currently in circulation are from 10 gourdes to 1,000 gourdes. Haitian bills or notes have to be the filthiest, dirtiest, limpest, most disgusting money you ever want to see or handle. Despite this, no matter how old the money is, it manages to stay intact. I imagine, especially in Haiti, Haitians are not concerned as much about how bad the money looks and feels; if it is not in your hands, it feels and looks even worse.

The Disappearing Cargo Container Contents

The year after I obtained boatloads of medical equipment and supplies from the old DMAT cache, I needed to find a way to get all this stuff down to Haiti. The Paris Twining Program of the Americas (back then called the Haiti Parish Twining Program), the organization helps churches (and even one synagogue in the Washington, DC area) twin with churches in Haiti. It also sponsors a cargo container program to ship medical and humanitarian supplies. We decided to ship by cargo container. Once we delivered the supplies to a warehouse in New Jersey for transport, that is the last we ever saw them. To be honest, it was the last time we saw the vast majority of what was shipped.

On our next trip to Haiti, we knew the supplies had made it to Haiti. We talked with everyone we knew and searched out every possible place, but we could not find any clue as to where they were. Naturally, we assumed they were stolen. At that time, we were staying a few days at the Solidarity Guest House in Port-au-Prince. While we were there, we were told about a clinic being run down the street for Haitians by a Catholic group. I believe the group was connected in some way with the guest house, but I cannot really confirm that. We decided we had some time on our hands, and it would be great to go on down and visit the clinic to see the good work that was being done. When we got there, we did see all the good work that was being done using a lot of our missing cargo container supplies. I could not miss the highly valued DMAT/US Army cots and stretchers. What could I say? I want my stuff back. I said nothing as I assumed as a best-case scenario that our supplies were now somewhere all over Haiti helping poor Haitians in need.

The Eco-Guys

No; I do not mean the "Echo-Guys." I really mean the "Eco-Guys." On one trip, we decided to stay at a new place in Port-au-Prince, near the airport, at the Eco-Guys Guest Grounds (my name) (no, not Guest House). A bunch of young Blan (I believe there were also some women) had come from New York City (from what I recall). They were going to save Port-au-Prince from all of its trash, waste, and garbage that still litter streets and especially the canals. In addition, they were going to turn a profit from their venture company. The most ubiquitous waste (not counting human body waste) is the plastic water and juice bottles and bags, either flattened by street traffic or clogging the canals so that you cannot even see the water below.

The Eco-Guys professed to be able to change dirty water into clean water, to process human excrement into fuel, and to convert all of the Styrofoam food serving containers into building materials. On site at the Eco-Grounds was eclectic housing: a tree large tree house, tents, a Quonset-like structure, and other unusually designed buildings. There was also a building on top of a dirt mound where guests contributed their excrement and urine for recycling.

When we arrived at Eco-Grounds, we were given a tour and then a presentation in the food processing kitchen. The host told us all about a process to clean up the water for drinking. At that point, I interrupted to tell our team that we only drink bottled or boiled water in Haiti. The host definitely was not too happy with my comment or with me. After the presentation, we were given choices as to which of the unique quarters we wanted to sleep in for the night. The host recommended one of the tents to me to use: privacy and a nice cool breeze. Once I got into the tent and closed the front flap, the air vents did not circulate any breeze. It was one of my most miserable, stifling nights in Haiti. Later on, one of my teammates told me to not ever challenge the host on the quality of his water.

By the way, one of our team members slept in the Styrofoam house. When she woke up in the morning, she had a Styrofoam rash all over her body. Maybe that is why I still see all those Styrofoam food containers on the roads.

Getting Through Customs

Getting through Customs in any third world country is not easy at all. Haiti is no different. Twice, we were not able to get our supplies through Customs and had to either cancel or delay our medical missions. Several times we had to find an open bank and get a cashier's check for a large sum of money to bail the supplies out of the airport holding cages. We have had to bribe, beg, cajole, persuade, treat, flirt with, and schmooze the customs officials to get our stuff through. As frustrating as it can be, you never yell or threaten.

We have learned and have used preemptive techniques to minimize the expected hassle:

1. The team members do not wear team member tee shirts as this links us as a team carrying medical supplies.

2. We use vertical duffel bags as much as possible rather than horizontal suitcases. Using these make the customs officials have to dig down deep to see what you have rather than trolling across a suitcase's contents.

3. We put the medications and medical supplies at the bottom, covered next by sporting equipment, and then topped by priest's vestments, when possible.

4. If we have a lot of medical supplies and drugs, we put the small containers of over-the-counter medicines (OTCs) such

as Tylenol on top, which allows the Customs agents to take their share of what they want personally, forgetting about the really good stuff at the bottom.

5. Since this part actually occurs in the United States when we pack the duffel bags, I can tell you the exact details of our most secret weapon to avoid discovery. After all the good stuff is packed, we lay pairs of Pat's panties, preferably dirty, on top. The more critical or crucial or costly the contents of the duffel bag are, the more pairs of panties are placed on top. This serves a double purpose: the more pairs of panties, the less inclined the customs' agents are to dig any deeper; the more pairs of panties we see at the top of the bag, we are immediately alerted on how hard we need to defend getting that particular bag through.

6. We used to go through Customs as an intact group, feeling safer in numbers. We just might all have worn those self-identifying tee shirts. Now, we try to break up and go though individually. We try to get the most experienced travelers though first to pave the way. Another technique that I have seen lately is to send the best-looking woman through first to roll her eyes at the customs agents. I never did suggest this initially, as some of the women figured this out on their own.

7. Pat will have someone already on the ground to work on the customs officials when we arrive. Sometimes this works, and sometimes it backfires. It does not work as well as in the old days.

Patient Patient Cases

No, I did not repeat myself. This vignette is about one patient Haitian patient. I could write short case studies, or vignettes, about each of the tens of thousands of patients we have seen over the past 20 years. Each patient would have a different story to tell. I have seen mothers and their unborn babies die of cerebral malaria; a baby, with a portion of his brain sticking out his skull, who I baptized so he could go home with his parents to soon die; malnourished children with worms crawling out of their noses; an adolescent girl who broke her leg the year before, with the bone still sticking out of her leg, weathered over the past year (the staff held her down under local anesthesia while the bone was reconnected inside her leg); a boy with his head cut open accidently by his young friend's machete; the breastfeeding mother with the breast mastitis with her breast so infected that it was the size of a large hard cantaloupe; the woman whose whole back was one piece of raw meat due to an infection; and the young father who came in with his jaw all wrapped (I thought it was a serious case of mumps, until we took the bandage off to reveal a jaw and mouth eaten away by invasive cancer; all we could do was give him the strongest painkillers we had and send him home to die).

I could go on and on. Instead, the story I will tell will be a representative one that describes medical and health conditions that Haitians, young and old, face and brave patiently every day of their lives. During one of our clinics, a young boy fell into the open fire, over which women were cooking food to sell to patients and caretakers. A young boy tripped and fell into the fire face first. He was badly burned. It reminded me of a very similar incident in the recent past where a boy with epilepsy had a seizure and fell into a fire. No medical personnel were around when that had happened. At least we were eventually able to give that boy medication to treat his seizures, which was a good outcome in that respect.

Fortunately, when the second boy fell into the fire, it happened right in front of the clinic steps. The man who was with him brought the young boy into the clinic. The doctors did what they could do with our limited resources and bandaged the boy. Even though the boy was in extreme pain and agony, he patiently endured whatever was being done to him. Once again, this reminded me of the boy who had his head cut open with the machete. That boy did not wince at all as he was being treated and his wound sewn back together. Though certainly not true for all patients, almost every patient who was brought into the clinic in the worst of conditions stoically and patiently endured the circumstances, as if it were nothing out of the usual for life in Haiti.

Now that the boy was bandaged, he had to be transported over the jungle mountain road to the hospital in Jeremie. As I looked out the pharmacy window, I saw a man carry the boy out to the road in front of the clinic. A dirt bike taxi pulled up. The man placed the bandaged boy onto the bike behind the driver. Then, he sat behind the boy to hold him. With the roar of the dirt bike ambulance, they took off for Jeremie. All I could do was look in astonishment. Everyone else seemed to look, or not even bother to look, at what just happened as nothing out of the unusual.

The Best of The Best

While it may be easy to dwell upon the hardships and misery of Haiti, there can be, at the same time, beauty beyond belief: the beauty of the country, the beauty of the people, the beauty of solemn peace and quiet, and the beauty of beauty.

Made in God's Image

To me, and I believe to many others, the Haitian people are a beautiful people. Due to the hard life and hard work, they tend to be mean and lean in appearance. Yet their faces, and especially their eyes, reflect back the softest and warmest glow. You see this in the faces of old women and men. You see this in the young girls with their perfectly combed hair enhanced by multi-color barrettes. They just melt your heart away. Haitian people seem to take an inherent pride in their appearance. When patients come to the clinic, they wear their best, and probably only, Sunday clothes. They wear them on Sundays too, when they go to church. The men will wear their best clothes, and suits, if they have them, even on the hottest and sweatiest days. Even so, I am continually amazed at just how cool these guys look all dressed up. The children who go to school wear their plaid uniforms every day.

I was blessed and honored to be chosen as the godfather of Benson's first child, a daughter, and for Mackson's first child, also a daughter. I remember the first day in church with those two little babies. Time flies. They are now beautiful Haitian teenage women. I see them every year when I go to Haiti. No matter where I am, they find me. As soon as I see them, I instantly look into their beautiful eyes and faces as the smiles spread across them. Then, for a while, we just kind of stare at each other. Then, I ask them how they are in Creole, and they say: Papimal. We talk for a while and then they are off. Before I leave Haiti, they are usually there to send me off. I would write more about this relationship, but there are really no words left, just indescribable emotions and feelings.

Haitian Houses

Haitian homes is probably a better term to use, but it is the houses that you see first from the outside. Unless you go in, that is all you will really see. In the cities, most are of cinder block, rebar, and slab concrete construction with metal roofs. There can be several floors in multistoried buildings. They are fairly inexpensive to build because of Haiti's vast resources of coarse gravel or crushed rocks such as limestone, along with finer materials such as sand. Unfortunately, this type of construction does not withstand the type of earthquakes possible in Haiti. In the countryside, you can see as many hut-like houses built out of bamboo, tree branches, straw, and banana tree leaves, with some fortunate to have a metal roof, as you will see cinder block houses. Most houses will have an eating area kitchen-type room plus a bedroom or two. Cooking, bathing, and bodily functions are performed outside. You may see some small gardens directly outside of a house.

Most Haitians that I get to know will invite me to and inside their houses. The young boys will take me home to meet their parent(s) and siblings. The adults will take me home to meet their spouse and children and parents. When I arrive, I am greeted by everyone living in the home. I am continually amazed at how many people can live in such small houses. I am usually invited inside for a short time to see the few honored possessions the family has. Then, we go back outside to sit and talk for a while. The inside is much too small and too hot during the day for all of us. I am not usually offered anything to drink (it would make me sick anyway) or to eat (there is just not much to give to me). I understand. We understand that I am not visiting or invited to eat dinner. We are together for the brief moment in time to exchange our thanks to each other and to wish each other well and to just be friends. I will soon be gone back to the United States and in this moment, time is very precious in Haiti.

When I come and meet the family and when I leave, I realize I have come to a home that just happens to be inside of a house. It is hard to describe the bond that I see that holds the family together despite the hardness of life that it endures. I know in my Polish family growing up, we stuck together, no matter what our family differences were. I have also seen families in the United States who have wanted for no material things destroy themselves just because of those material possessions. These families do not have homes; they are just human beings inside houses. Of course, no one ever knows for sure what goes on inside any family. I know Haitian houses are nothing like Polish houses. I do know there seems to be much similarity between Haitian homes and Polish homes.

The Farewell Parties

When Haitians have a reason to throw a party, the know how to do it up with their limited resources. When the medical teams have finished their work, it is hard to get out of Haiti without a farewell party. They are usually on the next to last day of the medical mission, that is, the last night before the last day we are at the clinic.

The parties start around 9 PM and can last for several hours. Some of us are so dead beat that we cannot imagine going to a party with still one more hard day to put in at the clinic. Our Haitian hosts truly want to show their appreciation for us with a specially baked cake, songs, skits, plays, games, and dancing. We usually end up as hot and sweaty as we ever will be the whole time we are in Haiti. We all go, although some of us try to slide out the door (sometimes even dancing out the door) after an hour or so. We are not always successful for different reasons. Mostly, it is guilt that we are not truly grateful for the gratitude that is being shown us. We all stayed to the end of the farewell party in 2015, though.

That was the party that the boys gave the appreciation speech and sang love songs to the ladies of the medical team. That is the party where I spotted and had my picture taken with the young boy wearing the "Nice" tee shirt. I never did find out just where he got that shirt. That was the party that was started earlier to make it easier on us. That was the party that had as many school children from Fosy's school as there were adults (maybe that is the reason we started earlier). When I came to Haiti this time, I brought stickers, a bunch of jump ropes, Frisbees, toy cars, bouncing balls, blow up beach balls, and five sets of baseball bats and balls from a friend of mine for the students and orphans at the school. I had given them several days before to Fosy to give to the children, but as of the party, I had not seen any children with the toys. At the party, I found out why. As I have said, Haitians are very resourceful, using everything and wasting nothing. Fosy has used the Frisbees and the blow up beach balls as hanging ornaments for the party. They looked great hanging over our heads. The next day, the children had all the recycled gifts.

At that party, a very special patient that we worked with on that mission showed up. It was a man who fell out of a tree and was completely paralyzed from the waist down. On our medical team was Katherine Irvine, a physical therapy student from the UMES.

Before I tell you the rest of the story at the party, here is a short synopsis of Katherine's reflections of the medical mission:

In May of this year, I had the incredible opportunity to travel to Haiti and provide help to people in need. I am currently a physical therapy student, studying at the University of Maryland Eastern Shore.

Upon embarking on my trip, I was told of Jean, who had been injured while harvesting crops from a tree. His fall caused him to be paralyzed from the waist down. In any society, this is a devastating accident. However, in Haiti, where medical supplies like wheelchairs and other adaptive equipment are scarce, and services like physical therapy are severely limited; devastating does not begin to describe the situation.

When I finally met Jean, I found a humble man who, despite his overwhelming situation, greeted me kindly. During our short visit, I was able to see him three times and offer him and his family exercises and maneuvers to ease some of his discomfort and make his life easier. I also examined several adolescents at schools in Haiti who had become injured in various ways. Unfortunately, many cannot get medical treatment due to the cost or lack of ability to get to a medical facility. I met with one teen whose childhood injury to his leg healed improperly from not being able to attain medical care. He was left seriously disabled, only able to walk with crutches for the past 11 years.

On our last day in the area, our group had the chance to enjoy some quality time with many of the residents of the area, including Jean. I had developed a feeling of despair by that time, wishing that I could have done more and wondering if my few days there were meaningless.

However, the gratitude and appreciation that poured out of the community on our last night was overwhelming. I was shown that the seemingly small impact I had made on the few people I encountered made a world of difference to them. I left Haiti a changed person, filled with gratitude for everything I once took for granted, and a desire to return to offer more humanitarian aid. After I graduate, I plan to embark on more Mission Trips to Haiti and continue to change the world—one person at a time.

When Jean came into the party room in a wheelchair while people were dancing, Katherine went over to Jean, took his two hands, and started dancing with him. Then, others came over and danced with him. How could anyone walk out of a farewell party like that, a party beyond belief?

Peace and Quiet

So far, I have said much about the noises of Haiti, especially its animals. The parties in Haiti are as loud as its music (try riding in one of those cramped trucks on a 10-hour trip with the driver blasting loud Haitian music on an endless loop). In the cities, the traffic noise of rattling vehicles and the belching and grunting of trucks rivals traffic anywhere in the world. Oh, also in Haiti, almost everyone lives outside most of the time. Get a good pair of earplugs may be your first response. That is quite artificial; plus, Haitian noises tend to get through any earplugs. In the cities, there is really no peace and quiet until you are able to fall asleep. In a way, that is artificial, too.

So, just when and where does anyone ever find good old natural peace and quiet in Haiti? The best time is when dusk has fallen before the roosters begin to crow. The best place is somewhere outdoors out in the countryside, preferably in the mountain jungle. You just pull up a chair and sit and feel the peace and quiet seep in, or you walk off into the dark and stare up into the sky or the far off distant unknown horizon, wondering what you are looking at out there. That is where you sense the deep peace and beauty that you see in all that quietness. You are stuck there with literally nowhere else to go, and you soak it in.

The Beauty of Haiti

The beauty of Haiti extends far beyond its people. Although I have been in only approximately ten foreign countries, I have been to all 50 states of the United States. Even if I had the opportunity to visit 50 foreign countries, I am sure no country would be more beautiful than the United States. By the way, my three most favorite beautiful states are Maine, Arizona, and Pennsylvania (OK; I was born in Pennsylvania). As I said previously, my first impression was of being in Arizona. So, how does Haiti compare in beauty from what I have seen in my lifetime? It comes close. I vote the United States number one by a hair. Those of you who have been to Haiti might say that much of Haiti has barren and grey hills destroyed by deforestation. It has seas with garbage and plastic bottles (oh, so many plastic bottles) floating in and out, in and out. The air is choked with smoke and grey dust and gasoline fumes. The rivers can appear that ubiquitous grey color, especially when churned up by heavy rains. Despite that, the underlying beauty of undisturbed Haiti can knock your eyeballs out.

On one of my medical mission trips, we arrived at night at a place in Haiti I had not been to ever before. We were doing a special medical mission to help another church. When I woke up in the bright sunny morning, my bed was facing a big open window. If I had been dreaming, I would have thought it was a big television screen, and I was watching a show about some beautiful garden spot in the world. As I looked out, I saw the valley and surrounding hills in front of me in full foliage with the ocean and then the sky making its backdrop appearance. I realized it was not a dream but beautiful reality, and I would soon be walking out and into it. There is a lot of Haiti that looks just like that. If only something could be done about the rest, Haiti would be the garden spot of the Caribbean.

Once we take our view off the ground, we then look up into the sky. We now know that the universe that God created for us has billions of galaxies with each containing billions of stars (suns). Living in the United States with light pollution would certainly give one doubts about those numbers. In Haiti, my eyes can scarcely take it in. Even in the cities, you can see at least millions of those billions. In the mountain jungles with the moon as the only light you see, you also see what seems like billions of stars. The sky is one solid mass of those stars. You get frozen in your tracks whenever you look up. Just when you think you have seen it all, God puts on one of His special shows. The last one I saw was something red passing through the maze of stars. Were they shooting stars? Were they comets? Were they asteroids? Were they red dwarf stars? I am not an astronomer and do not have astronomy talents to pick stuff out of the sky and tell you exactly what they were and where they came from or where they were going. Even when I got home and Googled red objects in the sky over Western Haiti on such and such a night, nothing came up. My eyes definitely did not play tricks. I looked many a time to make sure what I saw was really happening. All I could think was that God had made something special just to be seen in Haiti and nowhere else. Haiti and its people were very special to God.

I did not need the light-protected night skies of Haiti to see another dramatic show that God put on. We were returning from Carcasse along that tortuous winding mountain road. We had reached the ultimate top of the mountain rising up from the seacoast at the halfway point back to Jeremie. It had been a somewhat rainy, misty day with the sun darting in and out of the clouds. As soon as we got to the top of the mountain, we looked down at the sky (one can do that in Haiti) and into the valley below. There it was: a massive rainbow and then suddenly, a massive double rainbow. It stretched in the mist across the whole valley and stayed there the whole trip down the other side of the mountain. I was not going to get motion sickness on this trip. My whole heart and mind were on the scene in front of me. When we got down into the bowels of the valley, we literally were at the end of the rainbow. The only thing missing was the pot of gold, but who cared? I have seen many rainbows in my life, including double and even triple ones. I never saw one so brilliantly surrounded by mist that lasted for so long. Thinking even more about it, I realized I had never seen a rainbow from above the rainbow before.

How much more God-given beauty can the finite mind absorb? God was going to test my mind. There was one more show for God to finish His trifecta. It would occur in Port-au-Prince, of all places. We settled in for the last evening and night at the guest house in Port-au-Prince. I had finished supper, and the dusk was slowly turning into night. My bedroom was on the roof of the guest house. It was the magic hour of peace and quiet for Haiti, even in the largest city. I found a chair and the coolest, breeziest, and most obscure place I could find up on the roof (hey, the Drifters had even made a song about this kind of stuff). Where I ended up, I could have turned my chair in four different directions. Only one direction met the criteria I had set for the chair placement. I really could not tell which point on the compass I was facing. Evidently, it was East from what was about to happen.

In the darkness that had now arrived, I looked between several building tops to the hills of Port-au-Prince. All of the sudden, the distant sky started to light up brilliantly. Of course, it was not the sun, but it seemed like only the sun could do this to the sky. It was not a sunset for sure. I told you that I am not an astute astronomer. It took a few moments to really understand what was happening. The moon was as full as it could be. It was rising over the distant horizon exactly at the beginning of nightfall. As it rose before my eyes, it was huge! As if all of this was not enough, it started dancing as it rose. I was pretty sure that the moon does not dance at any time. Was the world coming to an end? Well, not this time. There were low-lying clouds floating across the rising moon that made it appear as if it were dancing. My mind was flooded with thoughts about the unbelievable, incomprehensible, most excellent, mind-boggling, masterful world that God had created for us made in His image. We had it right from the beginning. The Earth was and is truly the center of the universe, created by God in the perfect place for us to see all of His natural glory. Could Haiti just be the dead-on center of the universe?

The Heavens declare His Righteousness, and all the peoples see His Glory (Psalm 97:6: appropriately, this verse is the central verse of Psalms 95-100, which praise the triumph of God's Creation).

One More Story: The Super-Sized Bottle of Mouthwash

I have one story left that I knew I just had to tell, but I did not know where to fit it: the worst of the worst, or the best of the best. I decided to create a category just for it. This category will be: The One Story I Still Laugh The Most About." Please bear with me. Hopefully, it will be worth it despite the length of the category title. This story is about one of the members of one of our medical missions to Haiti. The object of the story will not be to identify the protagonist. I can tell you it is not the anonymous person in my other stories.

After crossing the bridgeless river next to Leon, we had to walk about a mile from the missing bridge to the rectory. The porters that were already carrying the Coke cases also carried our large bags. Before we go to Haiti, we are all issued the Haiti Travel Guide. A copy of the Guide is provided in Appendix 1 to give you an idea of what is like to prepare for a medical mission to Haiti and why we travel the way we do.

Here is one of the guidelines: **We ask you to pack as light as possible.** After getting to the rectory, we all unpacked. The team member opened his/her (I do not want to give any clues as to who this person is) suitcase. One-quarter by volume, and probably by weight, was this Costco Warehouse super-sized, last a lifetime, all-family bottle of mouthwash. Think five-gallon water jug but somewhat smaller. We all had a big laugh while the owner of the bottle sheepishly smiled. We were only going to be in Leon for three days and Haiti for seven days. This mouthwash had now already travelled across Haiti, and the plane had not crashed due to being overweight.

Here is another guideline: **There may be no electricity, so whatever you bring, make sure it is charged.** The next day around mid-morning, we were sitting on the rectory veranda talking with Pere Jean Antoine. All of the sudden, the rectory generator fired up and started running. The generator only runs at night for lighting after those nights when there was not enough sunlight during the day to recharge the ten 12-volt batteries in series (that equals the needed 120 volts). One of us asked Pere Jean Antoine why in the world was he was running the generator at this time of the day. We thought there might be some dire emergency. He replied that the owner of the mouthwash needed to recharge his/her shaver and asked Pere Jean to run the generator so he/she could do so. We had to ask Pere Jean Antoine quite diplomatically to please shut down the generator. Later in the week, we flew back to Port-au-Prince with the mouthwash and uncharged shaver. We are now back at the guest house. Water can be even scarcer than in the countryside with its flowing streams and accessible rivers.

The following guideline is not specifically addressed in our guidelines because it discussed on the ground in Haiti, and posters are posted at the guest house in the dining area and in the bathrooms. It is simply that water is very precious in Haiti, so you do things like take very short showers (if we are fortunate to have a cistern and shower: turn on the water and get wet; turn it off after and soap up; turn the water on again and rinse off; turn the water off). There are also instructions on when and how to use and flush the toilet (most Haitians are quite astounded that Americans waste three to five gallons of good water just to flush our pee).   By the way, if there is no shower, you use a bucket of water and a cup to replace the shower. You stand in a washtub and save the waste water to pour into the back of the toilet for the next necessary flush. Back to my story, once again there are several of us sitting downstairs with the director of the guest house. He hears the water running upstairs. Several minutes later, he still hears the water running. From what I recall, it was at approximately at the ten-minute mark that he bolted out of his chair and up the stairs to the rooftop bathroom and shower. The director was a former priest, but I am sure he used more than a priestly admonition, like Pere Jean Antoine would have. Do I have to tell you who the director found in the shower? I am not sure if the mouthwash was also there.

When we finally boarded the plane back to the United States, the infamous and notorious team member was somehow still alive, in possession of a charged shaver (not sure how he/she did it), and without the bottle of mouthwash. It was so big; it still might not have run out in Haiti.

Chapter 8

Final Thoughts

With a medical mission to Haiti comes a mixture of apprehension and excitement. With each trip, we encounter new challenges that we must overcome. Despite the hardships, however, we still continue to go back. Why? We forget about the struggles that we experienced during those long weeks and only seem to remember the wealth of gratitude that we received from the patients that we treated. We return home knowing that we made a difference in the lives of both the healthy and the sick. We know we have given them hope, if nothing else. There is no better feeling in the world than the emotions that we bring back home. The Haitian people's selfless acts of kindness and the appreciation that we get in return are what motivate us to return to Haiti year after year.

Every individual who personally commits his/her life to rebuilding Haiti is placed at a nexus of two competing elements: a country on the edge of catastrophe and the happiness and camaraderie that is still present in Haiti. Believing that there exists great potential to overcome the factors causing the struggle in Haiti and having faith in value of each Haitian's life are what influence us to continue serving the Haitian people. Most importantly, from our medical missions we take home beautiful lessons on love and happiness. We learn that true happiness that is satisfying and fulfilling comes from the intangible aspects in life. The Haitians teach us that true happiness is found in family, friendships, and genuine faith.

To the Christian believer, there are no coincidences or chance in our lives and in the world. If one thing happened outside of God's control, God would not and could not be God. I had just finished the previous paragraph as the last paragraph of this book. The words were to be my final thoughts about Haiti. God was not quite through with me yet. He had one more lesson to teach me about why I was not a racist in His eyes and why most Christians are not racists. I have just returned from the peace and quiet of West Virginia with no Internet and no television and only books to read. I have read every book on my large bookshelf in West Virginia, so when I am there, I rummage through to find a book that is worth reading again. This time I found The Wounded Healer by a Christian minister, Henri J.M. Nouwen. As I read the first several chapters, I almost gave it up as I felt I was not reading anything new. I decided to plug through and got to a section called "Principles of Christian Leadership." Nouwen was mainly speaking to other ministers, but he could very well have been speaking to us in Haiti.

Nouwen describes three basic principles of Christian leadership: personal concern, faith, and hope. Please listen closely to what he says about each:

1. **Personal Concern.** The great illusion of leadership is that one can be led out of the desert by someone who has never been there. Understanding requires sharing. God recognized that when He sent His Son to earth to become a man to touch the soul of a community. The suffering of the world is disturbed most by the distant lack of concern for his fellow man. What they really ache for is an attentive ear, a word of encouragement and support, a tender smile, a forgiving hug, a firm hand in theirs, or even just an acknowledgement of the inability to do more. Those suffering yearn for someone personally concerned enough to share his/her personal concerns.

2. **Faith.** This is faith in the value and meaning of life, beyond the face of despair and death. With this type of faith, every experience holds a new promise, every encounter enlightens, and every event brings a new message. Every experience,

every encounter, and every event become a direct appeal to discover and rediscover and search out each other's hearts. If one has a deep-rooted faith in the value and meaning of life, the Christian leader hears the cry for help behind the suffering. They are afraid to die and afraid to live. With this faith, the Christian hears the cry of help from the suffering, for someone to be with them not only in life, but also in death.

3. **Hope.** The deepest motivation for leading our fellow man to the future is hope. Hope offers a vision beyond suffering and even death. The Christian leader has been given a promise by God: a new life, even in the face of suffering and death. Hope allows us to move away from the safe place and walk the hard road to unknown and fearful territory. Without this hope, there is no real reason to become personally concerned or to have faith that there is light on the other side of darkness.

The paradox of Christian leadership and ministry in countries like Haiti is that the way out of all pain, despair, fear, confusion, and disillusionment is the way in. Only by us entering into communion with human suffering in Haiti can Haitians find relief. To overcome our neighbor's pain, despair, fear, confusion, disillusionment, and suffering, we must enter into it with him. In the fellowship of suffering, God will provide the way to freedom for the leader and the led.

Haiti is beyond belief. God is beyond belief. Bondye bon!!!

Epilogue

Dateline: February 13, 2016

1. The Last Trip Back

I am now sitting at the airport in Port-au-Prince. My flight to leave Haiti has been delayed as usual. Hurry up and wait: that is what one does in Haiti.

All of my travels in Haiti begin with great optimism that this will be the trip that goes as it should. Without that optimism, one would never venture out in Haiti. Nothing was different this time. The plan was to ride a motorbike from Leon to Jeremie early Friday morning, February 12 at 3:30 AM to arrive in Jeremie at 4:30 AM for the 5:00 AM bus departure to Port-au-Prince.

On Wednesday, February 10, the rains began to fall on and off. After one of the downpours in the afternoon, during a break in the skies, I was with the four boys at the orphanage. I asked them if it would rain again. Carlos spoke up and said that the rain was done for the day. Was he ever wrong. Several hours later, it began to rain harder and more often until midnight when it really broke loose. The rain now came down in waves of torrential bursts. It reminded me of Hurricane Agnes on June 20-23, 1972 when I lived in Northeastern Pennsylvania (fondly called NEPA by us coal miners). During Agnes, the entire Wyoming Valley of NEPA, including my hometown of Plymouth, had been covered in over 40 feet of water from one mountainside to the other and from one end of the Susquehanna River to the other. Rainfall was one inch an hour for 24 straight hours as Agnes crossed over NEPA, turned around and came back, and then stalled. The rain in Leon did not last for 24 hours, but it did continue unabated until 6:00 AM. At that time, there was a 30 minute pause, and then the next wave came. The waves came and went until 12 noon, Thursday, February 11.

We decided that I could not risk riding on a motorbike to Jeremie the next morning in a potential storm plus in the dark. With a break in the Thursday afternoon rain, I headed to Jeremie on the motorbike with a very experienced Haitian driver. It did rain on us occasionally, but the driver took the brunt of the rain as I sat protected behind him. Shortly after arriving in Jeremie and being safely under cover, the rains hit. It had not rained in Jeremie at all on Thursday or Friday morning. I had bitten the bullet, survived, and felt quite good about it. It does not rain much in Jeremie, at least not like it does in Leon up in the jungle mountains. I went to bed early Friday evening with a cool, fall-like breeze blowing off the ocean. I woke up at 1:00 AM on Friday, February 12, and heard water running off the guest house roof. That was strange; why would water be leaking from the house where water is not plenty? I listened outside though my window. I heard no rain, only the water running off the roof.

I fell back to sleep, anticipating my 4:00 AM wakeup call. Instead I got my wakeup call at 3:00 AM when I again heard water leaking, but this time almost hidden by a torrential downpour. It lasted about 45 minutes. I got up and packed to go to the bus station three blocks down the road. I decided to leave at 4:15 AM instead of 4:30 AM as I had to walk down a very steep, now slippery road, in the pitch dark (no electricity in Jeremie at this time). As soon as I hit the street, the rain started again. I would now get soaked along with my suitcase and duffel bag at the last moment. Right at that moment, a van came down the street and stopped. It was the bus owner along with her crew of employees. I got in with my luggage and made it to the bus station only slightly damp. I had bitten another bullet and was still dry; wow, was this good or not?

The bus almost always leaves promptly at 5:00 AM (exceptional and rare for Haiti). The bus driver was a little late this morning, though, and we pulled out at 5:10 AM, ten minutes late. The bus was rolling along, past places where I had ridden before in vehicles that had broken down. Could this actually be the first trip back home from Haiti where nothing would go wrong? We had made great time, and it was now exactly 6:30 AM. We rounded a curve and came to a sudden stop.

Sitting in the front seat next to the bus driver because of my motion sickness, I had a bird's eye view up there. We were about to go up a severe switch-back (S-Curve) with a deep gorge in between the "S." A large flat-bed tractor trailer did not make it past the lower part of the S-Curve. The thousand bags of cement bags held on by tie-down straps had shifted, and the truck jack-knifed. The back third of the truck was now hanging over the gorge; the truck cab was overturned against the hill on the other side with the cab crushed. The front of the truck was smashed up against the hillside. The only part of the truck not destroyed was the cab portion where the truck driver sat. He had crawled out the swinging and upside down door and escaped uninjured. The narrow muddy road was now blocked.

My bus was the first vehicle to arrive on the scene. It appeared that the accident occurred minutes before we appeared. My first thought was that if we had only left the bus station on time, we would have gotten there before the truck would come. That thought was quickly replaced by the thought that if we had left on time, we just might have met the truck just as it was flipping over. Our bus would have been knocked into the gorge. My next thought was of a big piece of machinery, as we see in the United States, soon coming to lift the truck out of the way. This was not the United States, and the only "official" vehicle that I would see was an ambulance that came later on the other side of the gorge, and then turned around and left. This was only the third ambulance I had ever seen in Haiti in my 20 years. Was the ambulance coming to check on the driver (good) or trying to get a patient to a hospital in Jeremie (very bad for the patient)?

The plan for the bus passengers was to wait for the bus coming to Jeremie from Port-au-Prince when we would transfer passengers and luggage form one bus to the other, but how could we get across the gorge (crawl over the flipped truck)? Two men appeared with a hoe and a pick-axe. They chopped down part of the hillside next to the impacted truck cab, wide enough for people to walk though and motorbikes to pass. The first motorbike appeared roaring though the mucky opening. We heard rumors that the Port-au-Prince bus would come to the other side of the gorge at 10:00 AM, three and a half hours later. It came at 12:30 PM.

With nothing better to do for the next six hours, I spent my time observing. You can always learn more in Haiti, especially by just observing. I walked up to the truck to see how close it had come to flipping into the gorge. Several men took two of the tie-down straps, tied them together, and then climbed the steep hillside to a somewhat sturdy tree nearly at the top to tie the strap around the tree. I was pretty sure that if the truck started to slide into the gorge, the tied-together strap was not going to stop it. Then again, this was probably not the first time this sort of thing had been done in Haiti.

Haitian people are amazingly resilient. Every motorbike made it through the muck one way or the other. Men and boys arrived on the scene to carry passengers' luggage and possessions for a fee. Taxi drivers arrived. Vendors appeared with those meals in Styrofoam containers. Messages travel fastest in Haiti by word of mouth.

Behind our regular bus there were several of those multi-colored, lumbering Haitian buses. After approximately five hours, one of these type buses appeared on the other side of the gorge. A migration soon began from one side of the gorge to the other. Going from our side to the other were adults and children and babies, goats, chickens, luggage, 55-gallon drums, huge washtubs, chairs, and assorted family and household possessions. Everything seemed to go over to the other side except the kitchen sink. Then again, Haitian hoes do not have kitchen sinks. Men carried three sacks of rice or two huge bags of charcoal on their heads back and forth, back and forth. From the other side came the same elements, except the goats and chickens were replaced with a mattress and a box spring carried by a small boy on his head on two separate trips. They all came through that narrow, mud-filled gap between the crushed truck cab and the steep hillside. Finally, at 12:30 PM, it was our bus's turn.

There was a nun on our bus, so a Haitian friend of mine, who was riding shotgun with me for my protection, and I helped her get herself and her bag across the narrow path. A young man carried my suitcase and my duffel bag on his head to the waiting bus. We were on our way again to finally arrive at the guest house in Port-au-Prince by 7:00 PM. My friend said to me, "In Haiti, life is difficult." At the same time, I was thinking, "It is not easy in Haiti." I nodded my head in agreement and simply said, "Oui." (Yes).

PS: The tractor trailer had already travelled over 60 miles on a road sometimes paved and often a cow path no wider than the truck itself. Did any of you wonder how one Haitian man, driving an 18-wheeler, even made it as far as the gorge?

2. Ford F-150

I saw my first Ford F-150 pickup truck ever in Haiti on the way back to Port-au-Prince. Being an owner of and driving a full size Ford F-150, I knew why. Mine would not last a month driving across Haiti. If we had not been stopped for six hours, I might not have seen this friendly pickup reminder of being back home in the United States.

3. Another Ambulance

By the way, I also saw another ambulance on the way back. Maybe, just maybe, there is hope for Haiti.

4. Polish Legionnaire Descendent?

One of the patients that the Nurse Practitioner saw at Fosy's school, but whom I did not see, was Paul Leexynska, which sure sounds Polish. When I go back, I will have to find Paul and see if he has blue eyes.

5. Happy Birthday (February 8, 2016)

While I was in Haiti, I celebrated my 71st birthday quietly with the whole country of Haiti and no one else. Bondye Bon x 71!!!

Appendix 1

Haiti Travel Guide

TRAVEL:

VALID PASSPORTS ARE REQUIRED. Visas are not required.
You will be given an immigration tourist card on the plane to present
at the Customs counter with your passport just after deplaning.
KEEP IT WITH YOUR PASSPORT. You **MUST** present it when
you leave the country. In the place requesting the name and address
of the guest house, put **CARCASSE. You will also be required to
pay a $10 entry fee when you arrive in Haiti.**

BAGGAGE REQUIREMENTS:

We ask everyone who is flying from the Washington area to put all
their belongings in a carry on. You are also allowed a purse/briefcase
which can be a large tote bag. We will need your check-in allotment
for items for Haiti. We ask you to pack as light as possible. There
will be several bags of medicines and other items needed for our
medical missions, which many of you will need to check in.

IMMUNIZATIONS:

You should take Chloroquine for malaria prophylaxis. You can
consult your doctor, travel clinic, or the Center for Disease Control
and Prevention Website on Haiti
http://wwwnc.cdc.gov/travel/destinations/haiti.aspx about additional
health recommendations.

EXPENSES:

All members of the Medical mission are responsible for all of their personal expenses. The major expense is airfare to Haiti. All money donated by St. Mary's in Barnesville and HEH is used totally for patient care and all of the costs associated with the Medical Mission, which includes medicines and hospital care for those needing additional medical care that we cannot provide in Carcasse.

Haiti banks no longer accept America checks so **make sure you bring at least $375 cash for in-country expenses.** These expenses include entry fee into Haiti ($10), bus fare to and from Jeremie ($30), transportation to and from Jeremie to Carcasse ($50), food and gratuity costs in Carcasse ($115), 1 night in Jeremie ($40), 2 evenings in a Port-au-Prince guest house ($90). Drinkable water will be available. If you want to drink either soda or beer, please contribute $1 per drink. **You must pay for all expenses with cash**. **Make sure you bring at least $375 in cash per person for housing, food, and travel expenses.** If you wish to purchase craft items such as Haitian coffee or rum, tack on additional funds. You should also bring your checkbook and a credit card in case of unexpected expenses, such as changes in your US flight schedule.

CLIMATE & CLOTHING:

Temperatures are in the high 80s during the day. Bring comfortable, lightweight summer clothes and comfortable shoes. **Don't forget to bring a bathing suit.** Carcasse is on the ocean. Most Haitian women wear skirts and dresses, although it is acceptable to wear pants, skirt-like shorts, or above-the-knee shorts. Please make sure that your clothing is modest.

CURRENCY:

The unit of Haitian currency is the gourde. There are five gourdes to the Haitian dollar. There is a varying exchange rate on American currency. Your US money can be exchanged upon arrival and unspent Haitian money can be exchanged back into US dollars before departing. Traveler's checks are difficult to exchange. **All expenses in Haiti must be paid in cash.**

LANGUAGE:

French and Creole are the official languages of Haiti, but most of the people speak Creole. A little Creole can go a long way.

SUGGESTED THINGS TO BRING:

You will want to bring a **FLASHLIGHT**, MOSQUITO REPELLENT, sun block, snacks for traveling. Drinking water will be available. **DO NOT DRINK TAP WATER ANYWHERE IN HAITI** (not even for rinsing your mouth or toothbrush). Bring your own professional equipment. For primary care people, this includes an otoscope, ophthalmoscope, and stethoscope. For nurses, EMTs, and paramedics this means a stethoscope, blood pressure cuff, and digital or ear thermometer. There may be no electricity, so whatever you bring, make sure it is charged.

ADDITIONAL TIPS:

Generally, the Haitian people do not have a problem with you taking their picture, however, if they say "no," their request should be respected. If you have any doubt, just say "photo?"

Unless you want to receive very expensive collect phone calls, never give out your phone number. If you give out your email, you will probably receive many requests for money.

Many people will be begging for money. It is impossible to give to everyone and especially risky if there are others around. Only give a small gift if it can be done discreetly or in private.

Your heart may be torn by the poverty and misery, which is very real, but you cannot right the wrongs and injustices done to these people single-handedly, and your generosity would spark an avalanche of people crying out to you and to others nearby.

We look forward to sharing with you the experience of getting to know the beauty and charm of the Haitian people. Our prayer is that you will be touched as so many have by the strength, resilience and the faith of a people who have endured unbelievable suffering.

"Our first task in approaching another people, another culture, another religion, is to take off our shoes, for the place we are approaching is holy. Else we may find ourselves treading on people's dreams. More serious still, we may forget that GOD was here before our arrival."

Don't Forget Your Passport

CHECKLIST FOR TRIP TO HAITI

PLANE TICKETS
PASSPORT--is your passport currently valid?
MONEY: **Cash (at least $375).** It is also good to bring a visa and checkbook for any emergency US expenses.
LUGGAGE--label your luggage properly
MEDICINES- that you may need
FLASHLIGHT
LIGHTWEIGHT SUMMER CLOTHING
SUNGLASSES, PRESCRIPTION GLASSES (or contacts and solution)
SUN BLOCK
MOSQUITO REPELLENT
WASHCLOTH/ LIGHTWEIGHT TOWEL
SOAP
SHAMPOO
FLIP-FLOP SANDALS (if desired for the shower)
SNACKS (for example: cheese and crackers, peanuts, granola bars)
CAMERA
EARPLUGS (to block out the sound of barking dogs, crowing roosters and/or snoring roommates)
BATHING SUIT
EMPTY WATER BOTTLE (fill up in US airport)
MOSQUITO NETTING FOR BED

LEAVE CONTACT INFORMATION WITH SOMEONE IN CASE OF EMERGENCY